Tempus ORAL HISTORY *Series*

Ely Voices

The Ely Link Road stone, and participants of one of Stephen's history walks for the Ely Festival Week in 1983 This, the original stone, was demolished on 21 May 2002.

Tempus ORAL HISTORY *Series*

Ely Voices

Nigel Billingham and Stephen K. Jones

Sevenoaks City Club, 1939. The Sevenoaks Road residents prepare for their annual outing.

First published 2002

Tempus Publishing Limited
The Mill, Brimscombe Port,
Stroud, Gloucestershire, GL5 2QG

British Library Cataloguing in Publication Data.
A catalogue record for this book is available from the British Library.

ISBN 0 7524 2600 1

Typesetting and origination by Tempus Publishing Limited
Printed in Great Britain by Midway Colour Print, Wiltshire

Contents

Green Farm which was owned by Harry Thorn in about 1900.

Acknowledgements

Thanks are due to all those people who agreed to their reminiscences being recorded in 1986-88 as part of the Ely Archive Project. All reminiscences, with the exception of recollections credited to groups etc., are individually acknowledged. Thanks again are due to everyone who originally donated photographs to the Ely Old and New Exhibition project. These people were all listed by name in the first two volumes. Our special thanks for the loan of additional photographs and assistance with this volume go to Sue and Phil Blain, Doug Erwin, Denzil and Thelma Gillman, Bob Guy, Gwenfô Gynt – The Wenvoe History Group, Mike Millward, Tony Powell, Gary Shellard, Tony Simmonds, Linda Williams, and all the staff at Ely library.

Introduction

Like our last volume in the Tempus *Images of Wales* series, *Ely Common to Culverhouse Cross,* this book also aims to take the reader on a journey – travelling this time through the memories and recollections of those who have lived, worked and experienced life in Ely, Caerau and Michaelston-super-Ely – a community known to everyone today as Ely.

Part of the work undertaken by the Ely Archive Project, a community programme project developed by Nigel and directed by Stephen, was to record interviews with local residents and others having a connection with the area. Recorded over the duration of the project, from 1986 to 1988, these interviews present an oral history that forms the basis of this book, together with older historical accounts and more recently recorded recollections.

As oral history it includes personal histories together with observations on the locality and the social and economic events of the time. In general it is not the well known or well heeled who are the subject of attention, but ordinary people. Here are the personal reminiscences of working class men and women – observers who do not normally leave memoirs or have biographers, and whose accounts are rarely recorded in official records.

It is a well-known fact that people really start to reminisce from the age of forty, recalling memories of childhood, adolescence and early adulthood. With any memory recall, the details of the event are greater depending on how significant the event or situation was to the individual. With such emotional events the possibility of selective recall may draw into question the reliability or accuracy of such statements. In the main such oral history, where it relates to factual information, has been found to be consistent with known facts. The important fact is that history is what people who have lived it actually feel and reflect about it and what we, as interpreters of this oral history, make of it. What we have made of it is the following account – covering memories of childhood, adolescence, work and relationships in youth, work and family together with recollections of major events such as war, upheaval and change in the Ely community.

As such it is not an account of high drama but a reflection of everyday life in an area that, from the outside, may look like any other city suburb and housing estate. Closer examination will reveal a diverse and fascinating history.

This volume does not detail the history of the parishes and industries of Ely, Caerau and Michaelston super Ely. Readers should refer to our two previous books, *Ely, Caerau and Michaelston-super-Ely* and *Ely Common to Culverhouse Cross*, for information and related photographs. In this book we have sought to use photographs that have not appeared in the two previous volumes.

In the last volume we raised concern for the built heritage of Ely, with particular reference to the loss of an historic building on the Ely Hospital site. Obviously it would be difficult to find alternative uses for building complexes that have now been swept away, such as Ely Brewery and the Paper Mill, but for other examples, such as the Ely Pumping Station and the Ely Industrial Training school (the original building on the Ely Hospital site), imaginative reuse could and should have been explored. It is not too late for St Mary's church, which stands, derelict and forlorn, overlooking its former parish of Caerau and the rest of Ely.

Shortly before the publication of this volume Redhouse Clinic was demolished, and a new B&Q Warehouse occupies the site formerly occupied by the depots and showrooms of Wyndhams, Finnings, Ely Transport and Rydale at Culverhouse Cross. Related to this development have been changes to the road layout, particularly at the roundabout, where it was necessary to move the Ely Link Road stone. This stone, which had to be demolished in the process, marked the opening of the Ely Link Road by the Revd Bob Morgan as Leader of South Glamorgan County Council (see *Ely, Caerau and Michaelstone-super-Ely*). A new stone of near identical shape, incorporating the European 'E' and the original plaque, will replace it – will anyone notice the difference?

It is our hope that contributors and readers will find the following to be an accurate interpretation of material, both oral and written – but please remember, not everything is as it seems!

Nigel Billingham and Stephen K. Jones

The original Ely Pumping Station building – built to supply Cardiff with clean water following the cholera outbreak of 1849.

1 Ely to 1900

Victoria Park early 1900s. The park was built on land which was previously part of Ely Common.

Mr George Thomas of Ely Farm claimed he was the last person who used oxen for ploughing and that he discontinued the custom in about 1850. When driving the ox-teams in the plough the men would sing rhymes, called tribanau, to the beasts. The songs were made up of disconnected verses each containing some topical illusion, mostly satirical, on local personages. Some of the rhymes were very coarse and were always sung to a particular refrain. A great composer of tribanau, often impromptu, was James Tubervill who was born on Ely Common in 1751. One of his tribanau was sung when he was ploughing on Ely Farm in the field adjoining Cowbridge Road. A group of girls were gossiping at the well, which then existed close by, when one of them threw a clod of earth at Tubervill. He broke into the following triban:

Mae merched glan yn Dwllgod
Ag yn Llandaf rhai hynod
Ag yn y Caerau aml rhai
Ond yn Drelai cleciod

There are fair maidens at Fairwater
And noteable ones at Llandaff
And many at Caerau
But at Ely there are only clackers

A triban was made against James Tubervill by Twm Llewelyn who sang:

Siemsyn Twrbil smala,
A godwyd ar y Cimdda
Rwyt wedi dysgu iaith dy fam
A hono gan y gwydda
Droll James Tubervill
Who wast reared on the Common
Thou hast learned thy mother tongue
From the geese

The following reminiscences of Ivor J.R. Harris were published in the *Cardiff and Suburban News* during 1952/53. Mr Harris's memories go back to Ely in the 1880s and have been, with only a few small omissions and the addition of headings, published exactly as he recorded them for the newspaper. Mr Harris was the son of the Matron and Master of Ely Industrial school (later Ely Hospital).

The rural community

I remember Ely when it was a small rural community, sixty to seventy, or more, years ago. Ely of Queen Victoria's reign! A village of serenity and quiet restfulness when Cardiff seemed a long long way off, with never a thought that some day – well there!

Oh memory! Shield me from the world's poor strife, and give those scenes thine everlasting life. Little did we dream in those days that Cardiff, the South Wales industrial colossus, would ever overwhelm this spot as it has done with its great demand for 'homes for the people'. It is only natural that I should touch upon the place of my birth.

Ely industrial schools

It was the Ely Industrial schools (now Ely Homes and Hospital) where my father and mother were master and matron respectively. Their appointment dated from November 1863 and where in due course of time I was privileged to meet many notabilities of Cardiff; the guardians 'of the poor' with others then interested in the well being of children. Across the stage they pass, Bassett, 'Waterhall' Farm; Geo. Thomas, Ely Farm; Alderman Ramsdale, Jacobs Trounce and Bevan; the Revd John Buckley, Vicar of Llandaff; Col. Hill and many more of that ilk. Of the under officials of the school there were Messrs Hess and Taylor of the boys section; Webber, Gardener, Miss Tiscoia, infants' department and Miss Brown, girls' section.

Methodism in Ely

The old Wesleyan chapel in Mill Road was a centre of religious activity in no small measure. Children's meeting at ten o'clock each Sunday morning was followed by the service at eleven o'clock. Sunday school was at three o'clock, with evening service at six o'clock and prayer meeting to follow. Often, however, this did not conclude the day of 'prayer and praise to God'; for someone or another would invite others to his home for a cottage prayer meeting. What strong faith and fervour these good folk possessed! We could very well do with some of it today.

Frank Bevan often attended to take a service, as did also F. Saunders. The Sunday school superintendent was James Bryant. He was a fine built man, elderly, with white hair and a beard. He was the timekeeper in the Ely Paper Mills. Then there was Simpson, a tall gaunt man of penetrating eye, yet withal of kindly heart. He was the bane of us, the Sunday school scholars. He was both a teacher

Old cottage in Mill Road. The end of the cottage was later to become Maud Horton's shop, which is still standing on the corner of St Margaret's Park and Mill Road today.

and absentee officer, and for the latter reason we knew him as 'the policeman'. It was only for him to get on his feet, and with arm outstretched would point to an unruly pupil, with an immediate good result. Presiding at the organ would be found either Messrs Williams, Smith or Miss Harris. Harry Smith's mother kept a shop on the Cowbridge Road facing the village square. He was a cripple, having suffered an injury when in the employ of Williams, 'the Mill' at the end of Mill Road opposite the old Pumping Station. This flourmill was driven by water wheel power. Messrs Dodd and Thomas were also teachers.

In going over the names of those fine stalwarts of Methodism, one cannot overlook Brown – George Brown – another Sunday school teacher. How well I remember him as a schoolboy attending Radnor Road, waiting for George Brown's lorry to claim a lift as far as the Ely Paper Mills. With what benevolence he would take each one of us in his arms to place us safely 'aboard'.

Travelling to Cardiff

And his horse! How we children loved that beautiful creature which seemed to reflect the lovely nature of the driver. To get to town in those days you either had to go by train or walk to Market Road, facing Alexandra Park, from whence a two-horsed car proceeded as far as the Pier Head. Lonely indeed was the thoroughfare from this point across Canton Common to Ely, particularly in the winter period.

On more than one occasion pedestrians had been molested. After passing the Ty Pwll Coch hotel, the rest of the way over the bridge though of no great distance, was desolation itself, with no lamps or footpath except a very crude affair opposite the mill.

SOUTH WALES RAILWAY.
TIME TABLE.—Sept. 2, 1850.

Distances	DOWN TRAINS.—*Week Days.*						*Sundays only.*		
	Starting from	Mail, 1 & 2 Class.	1 & 2, and Parly.	1 & 2 Class.	1 & 2 Class.	1, 2, & 3 Cl.	Mail, 1 & 2 Class.	1, 2, & 3 Cl.	1 & 2 and Parly.
Mls.		p.m.			a.m.	a.m.	p.m.		
	Paddington......	8 55	—	—	9 50	10 15	8 55	—	—
		a.m.	a.m.	noon.	p.m.	p.m.	a.m.	a.m.	p.m.
0	Chepstow	4 45	7 15	12 0	4 30	7 30	4 45	7 0	7 0
5	Portskewet.. ...	—	7 25	12 10	—	7 40	—	7 10	7 10
17	Newport	5 20	7 55	12 40	5 0	8 10	5 20	7 40	7 40
22½	Marshfield	—	8 9	12 55	5 12	8 25	—	7 54	7 54
29	Cardiff........ ...	5 45	8 23	1 10	5 23	8 38	5 45	8 8	8 8
31¼	Ely	—	8 30	1 17	5 30	8 45	—	8 15	8 15
40	Llantrissant, for Cowbridge ..	6 7	8 50	1 32	5 41	9 3	6 7	8 35	8 35
45¼	Pencoed	—	9 10	1 37	—	9 15	—	8 55	8 55
49½	Bridgend	6 35	9 30	1 52	6 0	9 23	6 35	9 15	9 15
55¼	Pyle	—	9 50	2 12	6 20	9 43	—	9 35	9 35
61½	Port Talbot.. ...	7 0	10 3	2 27	6 34	9 56	7 0	9 48	9 48
64½	Briton Ferry	—	10 10	2 34	—	10 4	—	9 55	9 55
67	Neath	7 15	10 17	2 42	6 44	10 12	7 15	10 2	10 2
	Ticket Platform at Landore..	*	*	*	*	*	*	*	*
75	Swansea	7 45	10 45	3 15	7 15	10 45	7 45	10 30	10 30

Train timetable for Ely, 2 September 1850.

Ely Bridge and Ely Brewery about 1900, from a watercolour.

One choice part of the village was between the river bridge and the station, where several majestic elm trees in full maturity divided the road way from a field, the latter in summer having a veritable paradise of hay, shaky grass and poppies.

The river

Opposite the Brewery lived Cross, the owner. This house is now used by the Brewery staff. Across the field mentioned was a footpath, to which access was obtained by surmounting a stile. This path led to St Fagans, and here and there bordered the river. To meander along this path in the summer was a sheer delight, with the slow flowing river, clear as crystal and stocked with fish and the banks glowing with reeds and marsh mallow. Alas to a great extent, those happy days have gone.

Danks was the name of the river bailiff. A man of whom poachers and youthful bathers stood alike in awe! Of somewhat rugged appearance, he was nevertheless good-natured, and a man of very few words, when on duty. [He was] the right one for the work. He was the perfect 'keeper' in his fustian coat, trouser and gaiters to match. Never can I forget how in round about 1885 he out manoeuvred some youths, including a brother of mine!, whilst they were having a good time down by the 'pipes' – or lower deep – as the spot was known. Like a bolt from the blue he appeared and at the right moment when the river separated the bathers from their clothing. I cleared off and from that day to this I have not learnt how the clothes were recovered by their owners.

Ely station

No bridge was provided for intending railway passengers to cross the lines, whilst to do so one had to exercise the greatest awareness to oncoming trains. Near the station was the Red Lion Inn and the Railway Inn. Both are still thriving. About the time of which I speak the station master himself was killed when crossing.

The present White Lion building was built in 1894 on the site of the original White Lion Inn.

Ely bridge

As to the river bridge it could in those far off days be described, as an ancient monument permitting only one line of traffic at a time, and 'humped' back it was truly a unique structure, of which there are not now many about. I'm afraid I often peered over the beneath, danced over shining pebbles and 'silver sand', emitting fairy tinkling, so parapet to watch an angler landing trout. The water in those days, as it flowed slowly captivating to him who has 'eyes to see and ears to hear'. Who can forget the mysterious youthful enchantment in 'looking over the bridge' in summer time!

Ely pubs

The Bridge Inn was a low roofed building with a privet hedge in front. Thomas Rees was the owner and his mode of attire was typical of a John Bull. His adornment was a low crowned box hat with a broad brim, his coat a swallowtail, which covered a light coloured waistcoat. With riding breeches and boots to match his appearance was indeed picturesque. He had two sons, popularly known as 'Tommy' and 'Johnny' and it was the latter, I believe, who took over the hotel whilst Thomas branched out as a contractor. Riverside Terrace was erected by him occupying the end house himself.

As to the White Lion the owner was named Moore. The house was, like the Bridge Inn, low roofed and with a wall, white washed, bordering the Cowbridge Road. He had a daughter and two sons, Edmund and Clifford, generally referred to as 'Ted' and 'Cliff'. The former was the first elected councillor for Ely, whilst Clifford migrated to the Midlands and became interested in running a racing stable.

Ely village square

In the centre of the village square was the remnant of the village green, diamond shaped, bordered on the west side by a cobble pavement, bordering the wall of 'the cottage', and occupied by the David family. Where a chemist shop now stands was a row of thatched cottages, about four or five of them, with front gardens, which could only be entered by getting over a stone stile. Between these and the river were several high poplar trees. Domestic water could be obtained from a well built into a garden wall (I believe it was the garden of a man named Stevens) and also from a spring on the edge of the river a little further up the road.

Cottages at Ely, 22 October 1888.

Great House

Great House, now occupied by the British Legion, was in the occupation of James Tucker, owner of Tuckers Flour Mills, East Dock, which later became tenanted by Thomas Osmond, haulage contractor, and owner of the quarry at Culverhouse Cross. Tucker often drove a tandem to business in good style and was a fine sight. When looking back over the years the following lines of Longfellow express my sentiment, for I:

See again as one in vision sees
The blossoms and the bees
And hear the children's voices shout and call
And the brown chestnuts fall.

Ely shops

In the row of small houses between the White Lion and Great House is a grocers shop where with other young companions I used to resort to purchase Chester cake and a bottle of pop all for the magnificent outlay of twopence. The proprietor was a man named Howard. These visits invariably took place on Saturday mornings.

Richard Williams

At 'Ty Lai', the cottage next to the White Lion, dwelt Richard Williams, brother of Christopher Williams of Red House Farm. He was a heavily built man and had an exceptional fine tenor voice. Often in those days did I listen with great interest to his rendering of such songs as *Sally in the Alley* and *Coming through the Rye*. An amusing incident is recorded of him when assisting the Caerau church choir at harvest thanksgiving service. At the commencement of the opening hymn he was observed to remain seated when other members of the choir were standing, and desperately wriggling to disengage himself from the stall in which he had apparently become wedged. It was only after great effort he released himself. He sat on the edge of the stall after that!

Ely cricket team

Of course Ely had a cricket team. Some of the members being; Messrs Hess, Taylor, Harris, Harrahy, Webber and Howard. Harris was the demon bowler and Harrahy the slogger. Yes there was splendid fun to be enjoyed at the matches on the Ely course where we played with the sanction of Farmer Emerson, Sweldon Farm.

Days of Queen Victoria

They were mellow days; tranquil days, those of Queen Victoria, and the summer was always as summer and winter always winter. In anticipation of the skating season, skates could assuredly be cleaned and made ready about the beginning of December and preparation for summer recreation commenced about April with every confidence that the weather would be the required kind. But now we hardly know summer from winter.

Cottage on Cowbridge Road

Opposite the Industrial schools – now the Hospital and Homes – was a two-roomed cottage in ground about four feet higher than the road and divided from it by a stream of clear cool water. One reached the cottage via a small plank bridge with a wooden stile to negotiate. The occupier was a man named Stevens, and upon his passing his remains were made the occasion of an Irish wake, and O! what a crying and wailing could be heard coming from the little home. I have not since then heard of a similar event taking place.

Stream by Cowbridge Road

Speaking of this roadside stream it was indeed the object of enchantment to me as a child and not only did it produce luscious watercress but 'fairy soap', that mysterious conglomeration so fascinating to a child.

Navvies at night

During the construction of the Barry railway the tranquillity of the village was often disturbed at night by gangs of navvies the worse for drink, returning from Cardiff or being ejected from inns. They were truly a rough crowd. The major portion of them came from Ireland and the local inhabitants were relieved upon their return to the Emerald Isle. Nevertheless they were renowned for their splendid reputation as workers. One night there was a gang of them passing the house about twelve by the clock, fighting and quarrelling. The next morning a dead man was found at Culverhouse and the incident was for many years spoke of as the 'Culverhouse murder'.

Ely Races

Ely Races was also an occasion for scenes of rowdyism and organised hooliganism. More than once I have witnessed a mêlée amongst rival gangs being dispersed by three or more mounted members of the Glamorganshire constabulary directed by Superintendent Wake.

One event affecting Ely Races concerns a rag and bone dealer named Timothy Donovan. He was a prosperous man and drove a mare, a superannuated racehorse by the way, known as the 'Maid of Killarney'. Timothy was a regular dandy. Tall, thin, wearing an expensive waistcoat, which set off a beautifully

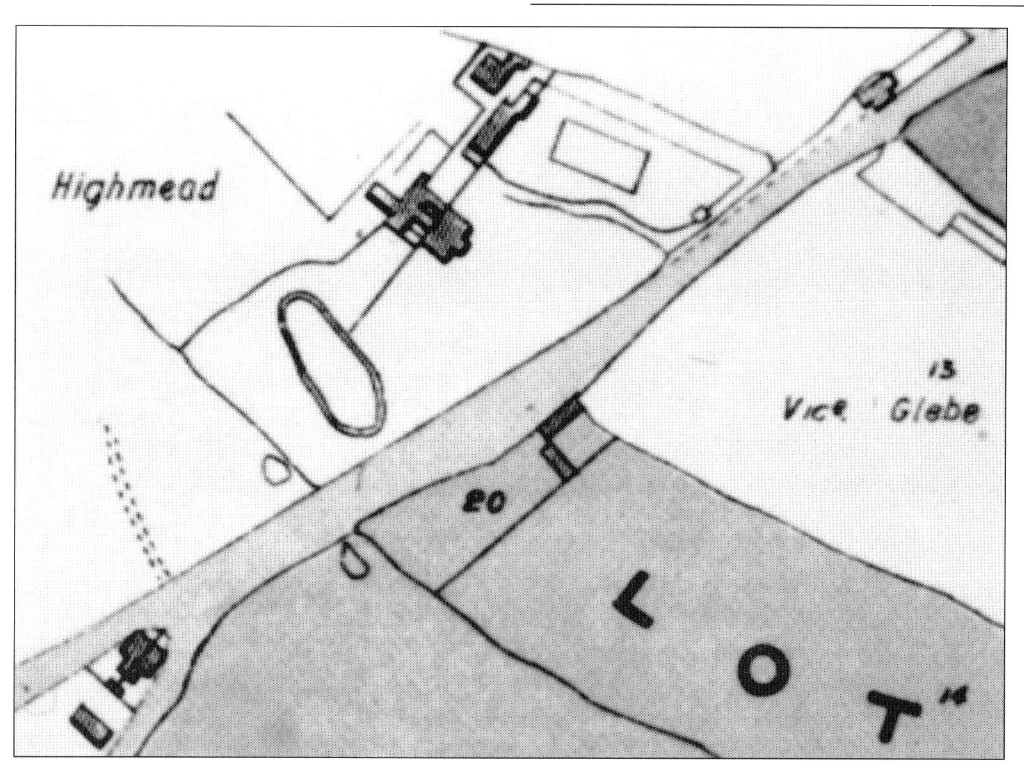

Map showing the tollhouse in the top right hand corner above Highmead House, from a 1904 Auction Catalogue. Bottom left is the current junction of Caerau Lane and Cowbridge Road West.

laundered white frilled shirt, his appearance could be called distinctive. Nature provided a comparison in his wife, who was as stout as Timothy was thin. 'The Maid' was reputed to have been a good jumper when in her prime, and there was nothing to do about it but for Timothy to enter the mare to race at Ely. The day came and for some unknown reason the stewards forbade him to ride so a youth was found to do so. At the start 'The Maid' was left far behind and was the last to pass the Grand Stand where I as a boy found a position near the first water jump, and the manner in which she cleared it was amazing. She appeared to stop for a moment, hesitate then reclining on her haunches literally sprang over. But would the old veteran clear all the other obstacles including the water jump near Ely Farm. Rather, for all the other runners had come to grief. Surely a classic race in more ways than one being the only horse to pass the post.

Ely postman

Between 7 o'clock and 8 o'clock each morning, postman Melhuish would deliver the mail, announcing his arrival at the entrance gate by blowing a whistle and then proceeded on his way to Bonvilston, stopping at various selected spots to deliver the letters and parcels conveyed in a small trap drawn by a pony.

Ely Toll House

Then there was Powell, the keeper of the Tollgate, who added to his somewhat meagre income by conducting a small general grocery business on the premises. One evening when passing the Toll gate with three young companions namely the two Elliott brothers whose father was stud groom to Mr Shirley, solicitor, and Johnny Benjamin, a son of Mrs Benjamin of the Dusty Forge ventured into the shop to make a purchase and, just as I was receiving attention, one of them threw a chinese cracker through the doorway. I found it convenient to retreat from the scene as quickly as possible and joining my friends a little further along the road. I found myself however in the unfortunate position of having to pass the Tollgate house in order to reach home, but saved myself from this dilemma by making my way along the other side of the hedge facing the house. For a long period I refrained from passing the Tollgate by road as a means of visiting Caerau but took the way of the fields.

Bowens Row

Where the Old Age Pensioners Cottages now are, was a blacksmiths and carpenters shop operated by William Bowen, who also plied the trade of wheelwright.

Constable Rutter

Ely of course had its officer of the law, Constable Rutter. He was a stout and muscular man, medium in height, and possessing an imperturbability of demeanour hiding an alertness of mind and body, which often landed a wrongdoer before the Magistrates bench at Llandaff.

Miss Jenner of Wenvoe

One of the most remarkable women passing through Ely seventy-odd years ago was Miss Jenner, sister of Captain Jenner, of Wenvoe Castle. My parents many times received a visit from her, so that I had a very fine opportunity of 'observing the peculiar make up of her apparel. She certainly was a woman of unique appearance. A narrow long visage bordered by a ringlet on either side with a small straw bonnet rather than a hat surmounting the lot. She wore a long and somewhat dirty black cotton silk kind of dress over which she wore shoulder cape set off with lace trimmings and was all in keeping with her footwear, which was as often as not a large man-size hob-nailed pair of boots. Sometimes she wore an over size pair of elastic side-boots. There were two things she was known to excel in. The first of these was her obsession for promoting lawsuits and the other her ability as a pianist.

In the former she continued suit after suit against her brother, so I was informed, believing as she did that he was keeping from her a portion of the Wenvoe estate, which she deemed, was hers by right. As to her pianistic knowledge I have heard her at my parents home perform most beautifully with all the eloquence of expression which became a lady of birth, as she truly was notwithstanding the oddity of her ways in later life. A story is related of her as having begged a lift into town from a passing cart driver. On arrival she gave him a small gratuity. Some time afterwards she summoned him for carrying passengers without a licence.

Redhouse Farm

Redhouse Farm occupying a prominent position overlooking several fields, which swept gracefully down to Cowbridge Road, was often visited by me particularly in the season of haymaking. The walk through the fields commenced where Grand Avenue links up with the Cowbridge Road. It was the residence of farmer Christopher Williams,

Gertrude Jenner in her house, Ty Pica, in Wenvoe.

brother of Richard Williams, who, on account of an injury to his leg, found a less painful method of getting about his land by way of a sturdy cob. If the gate opening into the Cowbridge Road was closed he would sit astride his horse until some passer by opened it for him. He had two daughters, years older than myself, with whom I on several occasions had tea at the farm.

On one of these afternoon visits there was a gentleman by the name of Seivier, to whom I was introduced. He became the husband of one of the sisters. In later years I was informed that he was a prominent racing man, and became known widely amongst the followers of this sport as a man who had made and lost more than one fortune. His full name was Bob Sievier.

The shepherd at the farm was an individual named Palmer, and in every way was as a shepherd should be. Well built and of somewhat striking appearance, he is the only man of that occupation who I ever witnessed carrying a shepherds crook. He was often to be seen attending his flock in a long low-slated building situated opposite where the pathway to Fairwater joins Mill Lane.

Keeping pigs

There used to be an old woman named Fanny, what her surname was I couldn't say. Dresses in volumous clothing after the Welsh style but minus the tall hat, who kept a number of pigs in the old barn in the lane, which led from the

Redhouse Farm showing both the old and new farmhouses.

Cowbridge Road to the Racecourse. Her head adornment was a kind of bonnet. Speaking of pigs there was Lock, who together with his other accomplishments used to kill pigs.

Patrick

One of the earliest personalities I remember was Patrick, another whose surname is to me lost in the mists of time. He had a club foot and when encouraged to do so would give a hop-skip and jump act along the Cowbridge Road, and what an exhibition it was!

Dennies Island

Another of my early day recollections is that of Regan, Patsey Regan, the acclaimed owner of 'Dennies Island', a bank of silt a few yards away from the river bridge and generally surrounded by water at intervals. But when the river was in full flood, Danny's pony had to be rescued from being overwhelmed, but no experience of this nature could disuade him from continuing to graze his pony thereon.

Highmead House

About fifty yards beyond the tollgate on the Cowbridge side was Highmead, the tenant owner being John Batchelor, timber merchant widely known as the 'friend of freedom'. A high white washed wall separated it from Cowbridge Road. On the front lawn was placed a life-size white statue. It could be observed through the iron gate, and often in passing the place at night its ghostly appearance bound me almost with youthful terror.

Saviger was the name of John Batchelor's gardener. He lived in Bowens Row, the cultivation of grapes being his special knowledge and many prizes were won by him

Above and below: The interior of St David's church before and after the installation of the organ in 1908.

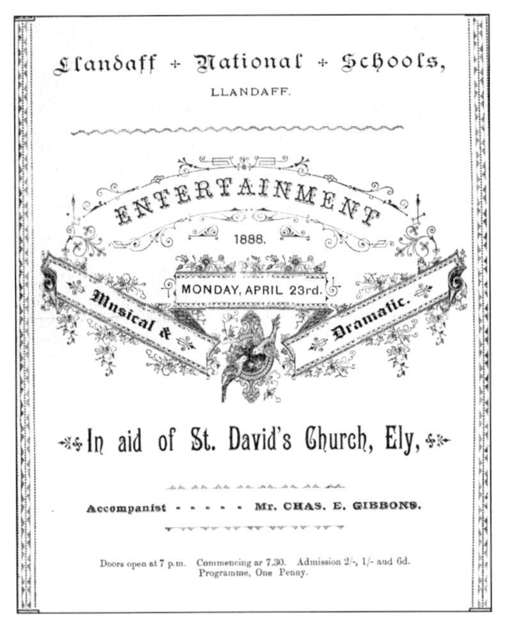
Llandaff + National + Schools,
LLANDAFF.
ENTERTAINMENT
1888.
MONDAY, APRIL 23rd.
Musical & Dramatic.
In aid of St. David's Church, Ely,
Accompanist - - - - - Mr. CHAS. E. GIBBONS.
Doors open at 7 p.m. Commencing at 7.30. Admission 2/-, 1/- and 6d.
Programme, One Penny.

Cover of an entertainment programme, which took place on Monday 23 April 1888, at Llandaff schools to raise funds for St David's church.

in local shows.

Rope works

On the right hand side of Ely Railway Bridge, on the Cardiff side, was Warren's rope works; a long low shed known as the ropewalk.

Reverend Johns

One outstanding inhabitant of old Ely, St David's church, was Vicar Johns. A man of simple, kindly disposition, his tragic giving way to liquor through grief at the loss of his wife eventually led to his giving up the living. He had one child, Trevor, a boy about my own age. Everything was his, which an over indulgent father could provide. We were much thrown into each other's company and were close friends. His youthful ambition was to be a jockey and his father had not only provided him with a pony but with a small jockey's outfit to meet his untutored vanity. He had ample scope for exercising his pet hobby for he had the racecourse near at hand with an alternative change of careering round the church grounds.

One notable event created a red-letter day in our association. It happened thus. Being of a delicate nature his father arranged for Trevor to have a part time tutor, who was in this case a nephew of James Howell, founder of the firm of that name. Now Bert, that was his Christian name, considered that pugilistic exercise would be of some value to his pupil and this led to a boxing lesson in which Trevor and I were opponents. The 'ring' was behind some high shrubs facing the church entrance and separated from the roadway by a hedge. When we were gloved my eager adversary outstripped the word go and registered a splendid bull's eye on my nose. The retaliation spirit worked quickly and somewhat disastrously. Throwing my right arm well back I brought all the strength that I could muster catching him squarely on the side of the face. Losing balance he slithered most unchampion like through the hedge into the ditch beside the road. The sight was most frightening and I fled from the scene nearly as quickly as Trevor's pony could gallop! Our friendship however was not endangered by this episode.

First post office

The opening of the first post office in the village was an event of some magnitude, the postman being a man named Lewis followed by Mannie Davies and then by Miss Dank, who recently retired from her position as postmistress.

Jimmy the fish

Jimmie Watkins, otherwise 'Jimmy the Fish', was a well-known character. He lived with

Janet his wife in the deserted 'weigh' office of the 'Alps Ore Mine' situated some little distance from the roadway leading into Cwrt-yr-Ala Park. He used to walk into Cardiff several times a week to purchase fish at the market for resale on the homeward journey. With Jimmie, however, money earned was easily spent, and often by the time he left Ely he was in a more or less befuddled state.

Tramps

Alluding to tramps, the 'community of the open road', there was never in my opinion one such as 'Jerry', again surname unknown. During his weekly summer excursions into the countryside between Ely and Cowbridge he would call at my parent's home to receive a mug of tea and 'summit to eat'. Often he would give me an orange but never without his benediction, 'God bless you'. Though a tramp he was much loved by many for his gentleness of character, and he was no ordinary tramp either, for was he not a gatherer of ferns, and herbs for some member of the healing profession in town. Did he not seek by this profession an honest attempt to find the ways and means to survive? At weekends he would hibernate in the Union, as St David's Hospital is now named, but in the winter he would remain there for the season. Then suddenly came the end.

An early or late snow storm swept the country, when one morning before day break, his poor weatherbeaten frame was found not many yards from the entrance gate of my home, covered in a mantle of purest white where loving hearts and willing hands were ready to have succoured him in his agonising distress. Did he pass on in an endeavour to reach my home? I wonder. This however I know to this day that a young lad mingled his tears with his elders, whilst men nodded their heads saying 'Poor old Jerry, poor old fellow' Yes, poor dear Jerry!

Pigeons

I have already made mention of Richard Williams, 'Ty Lai'. He was a man of leisure and interested in racing pigeons, having as an able assistant a man named Clarke. What these two did not know about pigeons generally was not worth knowing. A good story is told of Clarke (fictional, of course) that one day when seated on the corner of the river bridge he observed a strange pigeon flying at a high altitude. Then opening his coat pocket and giving a call whistle, the bird dived straight down into it.

George Thomas of Ely Farm

Another outstanding person of public notability was George Thomas of Ely Farm. Well known as an agriculturalist throughout the Vale of Glamorgan he also established himself as a historian of Wales. He was undoubtedly a brilliant Welsh scholar. To hear him declaim at various public and private functions, where he was always an honoured guest, was an occasion to be remembered. His oratory in both English or Welsh idiom was of a high order.

As a child it was a privilege to be taken to Ely Farm by my parents. The great man would place me upon his knee and in ponderous tone would tell me all about 'Ifor Bach' of Castell Coch, Llewellyn, first Prince of Wales, or other patriots of ancient Wales. He had three sons, Illtyd, Thomas and Teilo. Thomas was the rate collector for the parish of Canton. Illtyd was knighted and became Lord Mayor of Cardiff.

The Hess legend

The man Hess to whom I have made reference was senior teacher of the boys at the

TO

MR & MRS GEORGE THOMAS.

ELY FARM.

HAWDDAMOR Y GWR A'R WRAIG SYDD WEDI BYW AM HANER CANT O FLYNYDDAU GYDA EU GILYDD.

We the undersigned voice today to you both in this Address the heartfelt congratulations of hundreds of your friends acquaintances and admirers in the County of Glamorgan and all parts of the Country.

Amongst the subscribers is numbered the Lord Lieutenant of the County in which you have been held honoured and respected through all the long years up till your Golden Wedding. And to the Address have also subscribed Lords Members of Parliament and Public Officials who have learned to admire the unswerving integrity and high sense of honour which has marked your career to both of you since the memorable 28th of January 1843 when in the Grand old Cathedral of Llandaff your troth was plighted to each, joy and sorrow, pain and pleasure have come, but with strong firm hearts you have together "hand in hand" faced the rough and smooth and have lived to the "golden" age of ripe maturity.

The past years with their tale of public and private duties honourably and faithfully fulfilled are a rich treasury for those whom you shall leave behind you that they, following in your footsteps, may attain perchance to some of the loving reverence in which you are held by those who know you best.

And in conclusion may we express to you the fervent and sincere hope that for you with whom we are today celebrating a unique event there may be yet left many years in which to go in and out amongst those who today wish you "God speed" on your Golden Wedding.

Thomas Rees. Chairman. Richard Williams. Hon: Sec.
R. L. Bassett. J Russell Harris.
James Holden. Jno. H. Beale Lewis.
J. Jenkins Lewis. H. Osmond.
Frederick Raper. John Rees.
March 8th 1893. R. J. Winslow.

Testimonial plaque for Mr and Mrs George Thomas.

Industrial schools. Over six feet in height with a shock of black hair and bushy eyebrows to match, he was a striking personality. He oft would catch hold of me and playfully bump my head against the ceiling. One day my father had to reprimand him informing him at the same time that it would be necessary for him to report the matter to the Board of Guardians.

The incident must have been of a serious nature for within a very short time he suddenly left without informing anyone of his intention to leave. In later years I heard my father express an opinion that he was a German spy. I further was informed that during his appointment as schoolteacher he was one day visited by his mother, a German, who had come direct from Germany. My eldest sister was introduced to her.

During the last war when Hitler attempted to enslave Europe, not forgetting England, a man alighted from an airplane, his name was Hess, and a photograph of the individual was published in the press. His face bore a startling likeness to a certain man whom I knew years ago and who had the same name. When I further remembered that this person when he left Ely was rumoured at the time to have gone abroad to Egypt, I concluded that the parachutist was a relative, in all probability a son of the ex-school master, as he was also reported during his trial to have resided if not actually been born, in Ely.

[Author's note: this story is something of a local legend but there appears to be no substance in it, according to recent biographies of Rudolf Hess.]

Ely Industrial School

Let me now conclude my Old Ely reminiscences by referring to an incident of which I was a witness. It relates primarily to my mother. It was a lovely summer evening, when from the field of hay opposite, or maybe of corn, the cry of the corncrake, a frequent visitor in those days, could be heard harmonising with the country atmosphere round about.

It was customary on such evenings for my father, with two or three male officers, to pass

Ely Hospital in 1983.

a couple of hours in quiet conversation seated outside the entrance hall of the Institution. As they were doing so on this occasion an ill-humoured tramp came through the open gate and advanced up the path towards them. Very quickly for some reason or another, he developed a threatening attitude, continuing to do so for some time with neither one nor other of the officials including my father, taking action to eject him from the premises.

Then it was that my mother came upon the scene and quickly summed up the position. Grasping one of the tramp's hands, she adroitly swung him round, then having secured both arms behind his back she ran him down the path and threw him on to the road; she had learnt the art of self defence when, as a young woman, she was a nurse at Bridgend Asylum.

My theme is at an end! Over the years the 'happy fields' of youth have merged with the happier fields of wisdom, with tranquillity, the 'golden age' of human life where each one may see afar off the 'city of the great king' built upon 'Kings incredible.'

Ivor J.R. Harris

Ely Paper Mill

When I came in February 1880 the staff consisted of Mr Smart, Mr Pratt-Wakeford, a junior, and Mr Bryant the timekeeper. Incidentally I may mention I had the honour of being the first shorthand writer they had here.

The distance from the town to the mill in those days appeared long and was a tiresome journey. A slow two-horse bus might be had

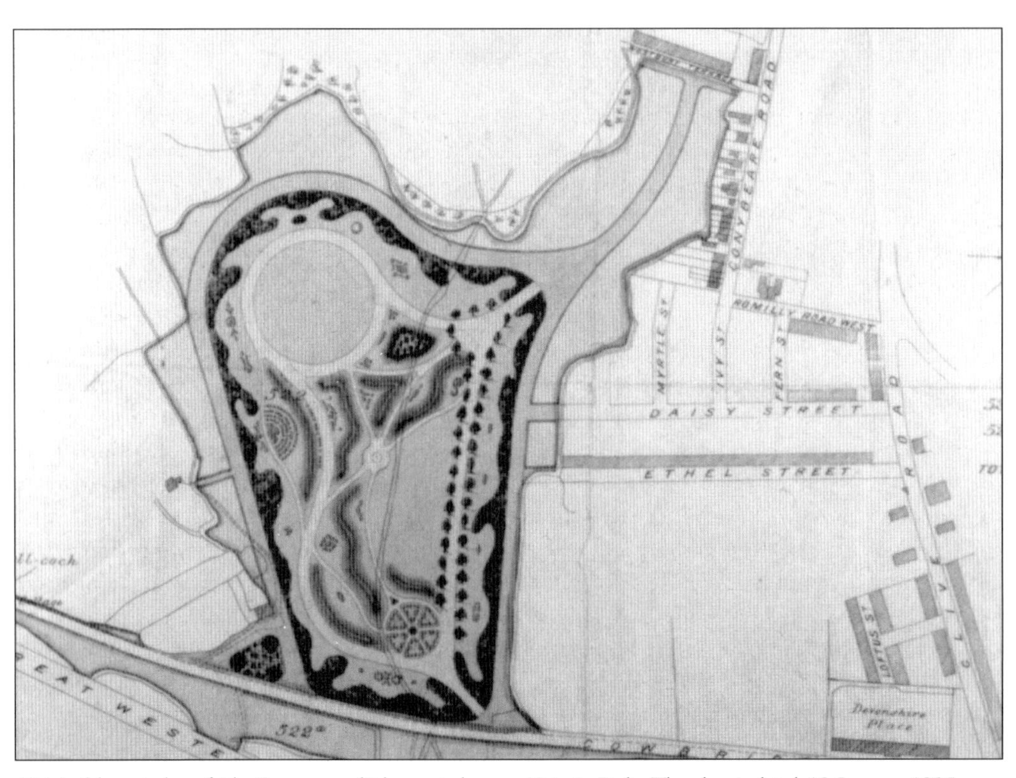

Original layout plan of Ely Common, which was to become Victoria Park. The plan is dated 19 January 1885, using the 1875 Cardiff Improvement Plan.

Ely Hospital (formerly Ely Industrial Training school) awaiting demolition in January 1999.

from the corner of High Street to Llandaff. Later came the one-horse tramcar. There were no houses on the right from Clive Arms, with the exception of Griffiths, to the mill, and on the left it was all garden with the exception of Goodfield's and Stanley's, from what is now Alexandra Road to the mill.

Crossing the bleak common was an unpleasant ordeal, especially in bad weather. At night more so, as there were no lamps then, or proper footpaths. It was a case of up and down – jumping the channels made to drain the water off the roads. Victoria Park was a wild barren waste common with a pond in the centre. It was common land to which the people had a right and everyone around who owned quadrupeds of any sort turned them out and it was a great boon. Being near the town it was never free of gypsy caravans.

Rags and esparto grass were the mainstays of the raw materials used at the mill but oat and rye straw bought from farmers for miles around was used. Afterwards the firm acquired a mill at Raamsdonk in Holland and regularly sent straw pulp for use in Wales. It was sent fairly moist and very good stuff it was, Dutch straw being longer, coarser and stronger than the native variety. Bombay hemp was also tried but proved unsuccessful. At another time flax was used. The farmers in the Vale of Glamorgan were encouraged to grow it and a large gentleman farmer in Monmouthshire was given a three-year contract to supply all he could grow. It was a source of great profit to the growers as they derived double profit – a good price for the flax and the seed into the bargain. Which was very profitable. Before the three years were up it was abandoned as several great ricks rotting down in the field testified. It proved too strong and stubborn a fibre and the cost of working it was too great.

Recollections of a Paper Mill employee as recorded in the Wiggins Teape Journal

Sweldon Farm

The original farmhouse dates back to the 1600s but it burnt down, and a cottage that had been built at the same time was used as the farm. Our families' involvement with the farm dates back to 25 April 1875, when William Emerson moved there from Fairwater Farm in Castletown. I still have the bible that was given on that date. It says William Emerson born in 1846 and married Cecilia Jones in 1874, and died in 1919.

William Emerson was very active in the church at Saintwell and he was also a staunch Liberal; Lloyd George visited the farm once. William also established a Hay and Corn Merchants in Severn Road, Canton. At one time William had to deal with a strike by the farm hands – they refused to milk the cows until their demand for a shilling a week rise was granted. They were offered sixpence and they accepted that.

In Sideland Field, just across the lane from the farm, there were roman remains. In my father in law's day they used to walk sheep to Barry Island where they had grazing land. They also used to walk cattle to Herbert Thomas's market in Ely.

My father in law, Rolfe Emerson, was the youngest of Williams's four sons. He also had a daughter, Ethel. Rolfe was born in 1883, married in 1910 and died in 1955.

Mrs E.M. Emerson

Find the Lady at Ely Races

Ely Races was then a very much more popular institution than it is today, and was always looked forward to from one year to the other, when I and almost everybody made a pilgrimage by rail or road to the racecourse. I had been working nights, and consequently had my day off, when I made my first appearance on any racecourse.

I had managed, by very careful saving up my pennies for some months, to accumulate the sum of a gold sovereign and a few coppers. These were stowed away carefully in an inner pocket of my waistcoat, as I had heard of the wonderful methods of the racecourse fraternity in abstracting coins from almost anywhere. I had made up my mind that I was not to be had in that way. On the side of the course was a man on his knees, displaying three innocent looking playing cards on the grass in front of him. A few yokels were around, very much 'interested' in this particular game, and, never having seen such a thing before, I also became interested. The gentleman on his knees said, 'Ere's three little cards. And one on 'em is the Queen of Diamonds', then, dexterously and with one hand, picked up the three cards, and let them fall with a peculiar twist on to the grass saying at the same time, 'Now he's 'ere, now he's there; I bet a crown to a bob that nobody will spot the lady'.

I became more interested when one of the yokels took out a five-shilling piece and of course spotted the wrong card and therefore lost. This went on for some time and I felt great commiseration for the loser as I had watched that the 'Lady' had always a turned up look on one of the corners so I felt very proud of my ability in this important discovery. I could see where the 'correct' card was every time and ventured to advise one of the yokels accordingly. 'Why don't yer 'ave arty yerself?' says the trickster. 'Wot'll ye bet? A pound' he says. I was cock-sure so I hauled out my solitary sovereign and – lost. He had turned up the corner of one of the cards and levelled that of the 'Lady' and thus I was cured of ever joining in a sporting game from that time to this.

S.W. Allen, from his 'Reminiscences …'
Cardiff, 1918

2 Before the First World War

Ely Methodist church in 1912, soon after the opening. It replaced the original chapel in Mil Road, and its gardens were shortened in 1924 to widen the main road.

Ely Wesleyan

A little higher up Mill Road was a big house built off the side of the road where Mr and Mrs Thomas lived. They were good folk to the chapel and when they moved to the Woodlands, up where Caerau Hospital is, our Sunday school often used to go there. Higher up Mill Road was our dear little chapel. The chapel was our life and Band of Hope was looked forward to each week. In the chapel was a round iron stove and one Sunday they made the fire so big that it caught the roof alight, but there was no damage done, the men soon put it out.

A well remembered family in Ely was Mr John Palmer and his sons; they were gardeners and wonderful chapel folk. Our whole life was the chapel. When we came from the chapel in Mill Road to the Methodist chapel it was a big day and we had a lot of well-known preachers and workers. Alderman C.F. Saunders, Paul Fairweather and Captain Harris to name a few. Then we had a big revival meeting led by Mr Massey. We had many folk converted. Old George Brown was one. He shouted hallelujah and put ten shillings in the collection – it was talked about for days. My grandfather was the first corpse they carried in there, the chapel was our life.

The folk of Ely could get work easy in Chivers, the Brewery or the Mill. The manager of Chivers was our Sunday school superintendent, Mr Alfred Smith, he was wonderful and when we went to chapel we had to sit quiet and not talk because it was God's house. To me my past was wonderful because I had my family around me.

Nora Coulson (née Woolven)

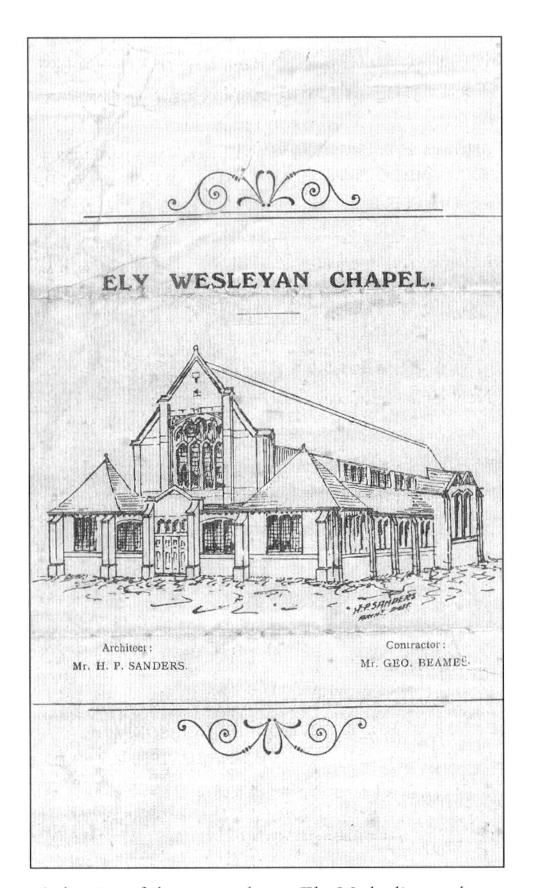

A drawing of the proposed new Ely Methodist on the foundation stone laying programme 11 November 1910.

Ely Post Office and Mill Road

I was born in 6 Cowbridge Road, Ely, in 1903, next door to the post office but it was not a post office like it is today. It was kept by Mannie Davies and his wife, the part of the shop in Mill Road was a butchers, the front of the shop was a grocers, and sweet shop and the post office was a small room at the back of the shop. A little way up Mill Road was a lane – it is still there by the greengrocer's shop, and down there was a tiny cottage where Granny Bridges lived. She was a dear and living so close to the river she was often flooded and as she kept chickens she used to take them upstairs with her, the cottage was pulled down after she died. Opposite the lane was a big dark house where Mr and Mrs Price lived. He was a tall man and always had brown dogs with him. He told me once I had a hole in my stocking and to go home and mend it. As children we used to go to their house to buy halfpennies worth of apples and used to get quite a lot.

Nora Coulson (née Woolven)

I used to pump the organ when I was twelve in the old chapel in Mill Road. I remember the service in memory of the Titanic. It was crowded out.

Ed Woolven

Ely Brewery

I was born in 1898, and joined the brewery in 1912 at the age of fourteen. My first job was as a stable boy looking after five big brewery horses. By the time I joined up in 1915 I had moved to the bottling department at seven shillings and sixpence per week. My hours were half past six in the morning until five, and a half-day on Saturdays. When I returned from the army I worked in the cask wash house and from the Second World War on as a shift worker.

I was not fully-grown as a fourteen-year-old and I could walk underneath the big horses. My job involved feeding the horses, attending to new straw for their bedding and polishing the brasses. I had to do all this before breakfast. Then I would go with a driver on a delivery and hold the horse's head when we got there. The driver would take lunch in the pub while I stayed outside and had stone ginger brought to me.

Ernest Strong

We would go to Ely Brewery for a 1d of balm to make herb beer, and we had to go to the station yard to buy our coal and push it home in a little truck.

Nora Coulson (née Woolven)

Councillors

We had two councillors in Ely, Mr Thomas Rees, who owned Riverside Terrace and the Bridge Inn and he was a Liberal, and Mr Edmund Moore who was a Conservative, who owned Windsor Terrace and the White Lion. Voting day was a big excitement because who ever won you could get free beer from their pubs. The Moores lived next door to the White Lion and Mrs Moore was my godmother and her sister Miss Ashton was my twin sister's godmother.

Nora Coulson (née Woolven)

Ely Brewery workers at the outbreak of the First World War.

WHITE LION HOTEL, ELY, NEAR CARDIFF.
SALE OF HOUSEHOLD FURNITURE AND EFFECTS.

MR. PERCIVAL J. THOMAS has been favoured with instructions by Mr. E. J. Moore, who is leaving, to SELL by PUBLIC AUCTION, on the Premises as above, on WEDNESDAY, August 11th, at 2.30 o'clock in the Afternoon, the Surplus

HOUSEHOLD FURNITURE AND EFFECTS,

Consisting of SUPERB SHERATON INLAID CABINET and OVERMANTEL, WALNUT SIDEBOARD, MAGNIFICENT WALNUT BEDROOM SUITE, MAHOGANY DINING-TABLE and other Tables, excellent PIANOFORTE by THOMPSON and SHACKELL, Old Oak Chest, Bedsteads, 7 Feather Beds, INTERNATIONAL AUTOGRAPH TIME RECORDER, VERY VALUABLE SET OF SHEFFIELD PLATE MEAT COVERS, 2 Clocks, Empire Typewriter, 18 Galvanised Buckets (nearly new), Quantity of China, Pictures, Spirit Jars, and numerous other Lots; 1 Safe and Stand, 2ft. 10in. by 1ft. 10in., by Thomas Skidmore; 2 Brass and other Fenders, 2 Hall-stands, Axminster and other Carpets.

Goods on View Morning of Sale.

Auctioneer's Offices, 18, Queen's-chambers, Queen-street, Cardiff. k1135

CROSS GATES, PENYBONT STATION.

Advertisement for the sale of Mr Moore's effects at the White Lion, 9 August 1920.

Williams family

Next to the big house lived Mr and Mrs Williams who were big workers in the Ely church. They had a son Vaughan who was a wonderful pianist and it was said he played for Ivor Novello. Next to that was a little house where old Daddy Howard lived and he used to bake bread in a stone oven out the back and he used to make toffee and peppermints. He was exactly like Father Christmas and loved us children.

Nora Coulson (née Woolven)

The White House and Osmonds Yard

Then there was a big house we called the White House, another family of Williams lived there but they did not mix much with

The view from just beyond Ely Methodist church looking up Cowbridge Road (West) towards St David's church in the distance, c. 1910-12.

Ely folk, they were too posh, so we did not see a lot of them. Next to the White House was Osmonds Yard where my dad worked as a blacksmith. He had a huge fire and I used to have to go there and sit on a box and work the bellows up and down to keep the fire going.

Nora Coulson (née Woolven)

Windsor Terrace

Coming to Windsor Terrace where the fish shop is, Sammy Loud and his sister kept a little meat shop and used to make faggots and peas and one day they soaked peas in a brown earthenware bowl and half Ely was poisoned. Dr Campbell was in and out of the houses; the poison came out of the glaze on the bowl. Mr Bowen lived next door and grew lovely roses. In the little shop next door was Mr Harry Smith. The shop kept everything you could think of and he was the organist of our Wesleyan chapel and all the men in my family pumped the organ.I think the last one was my son Mervyn.

Nora Coulson (née Woolven)

St Mary's church

Our outings were taking our tea up to Caerau and sitting on the tump to eat it, and as all our family are buried up there we had a lot of graves to see to. There was a lovely family living in Caerau by the name of Mr and Mrs Vivian and before Palm Sunday every grave was tidied up and flowers put on them. A funeral in Ely was a big occasion, they used to congregate in the square and sing hymns and then go onto Caerau. They were carried up the hill because the horses could not get up there.

Nora Coulson (née Woolven)

Deliveries

We had a vegetable man come once a week called George Hilborne and Gertie Bond used to deliver milk every day. We had to take our jugs to the cart and she would dip the milk out of a big churn. We could also get our milk from a dear little lady, Miss Edding, in the last house in Mill Road. Charlie Luke used to come with his bakers-cart once a day.

Nora Coulson (née Woolven)

Ely races

Our big day was race day and we used to mind bikes in our fronts and when they came to collect their bikes you could tell who won by what they gave you. Sometimes you would get 6d but more often than not it was 1d or 2d. The racecourse was behind the allotments and we used to go with Dad, and by the hedge was the water jump and we had to be quiet when they came to the jump and as they jumped we were splashed with water. After the races we

St Mary's church, Caerau taken in 1945.

Ely Bridge at the turn of the century.

used to go through the hedge into the racecourse up into the stands to see what we could find and we had money, empty bottles, cigarette cards and sometimes coats. They were good days.

Nora Coulson (née Woolven)

On the Parish

When my granddad died my Gran had to walk to Llandaff for 4 shillings parish pay and she had to struggle to make ends meet but neighbours were good to help each other and nobody had a locked door. You could go into anybody's house because we all knew each other.

Nora Coulson (née Woolven)

The Toll House

Up Cowbridge Road just past the Dager was a little stone cottage where old Mr Fowler lived. They said it was the toll man's cottage. He was lovely – we would go up there and ask him for a drink.

Nora Coulson (née Woolven)

Ely River

If we wanted to know anything we had Mr Eastern who lived in Wroughton Place, he would always help you. He was a fisherman. Also old Daddy John in Riverside Terrace; the two spent a lot of time together. There were quite a few folk drowned in Ely River including my uncle Frank aged nine.

Nora Coulson (née Woolven)

Nurse Willis

I must not forget Nurse Willis. She brought all of us into the world, there were no clinics then, nature had its own way.

Nora Coulson (née Woolven)

Robert Street and Riverside Terrace

When they put up new houses in Robert Street, one Sunday we had a terrific gale and one house was blown down. There was no Clarke Street - it was a big field called Harry Smiths. We used to have fairs and roundabouts at the bottom of Robert Street. It was exciting.

Riverside Terrace was built in 1886 and when we went there in 1909 we had one tap behind the back door, and had to carry water out to the lavatory and at the bottom of each garden was a stone stile, which led to a well in the yard at the bottom of the terrace.

Nora Coulson (née Woolven)

Number 6 Riverside Terrace.

Dusty Forge

I wonder if there is more life and love in a village than in a town. Ely ended at the Dusty Forge and in one of my books I have the story of the devil going to the Dusty Forge for a new hoof but before they could put it on the cock crowed and he ran away.

Nora Coulson (née Woolven)

Floods

I must not forget to say about the floods and what we suffered. Once it was so bad that Mr Brain of Cwrt-yr-Ala sent a boat and passed up a pint of milk and a loaf to folk upstairs. We had a dreadful mess to clean up after. We had a lovely swan on the river for years, we called him Billy, he used to come and knock our door with his bill every morning and we fed him. Once he came in the house and we had a job to get him out until he had a crust of bread. Then he went back to the river quite happy.

Nora Coulson (née Woolven)

Wedding disappointment

When anybody got married we used to tie the gate and not undo them until they threw us half or one penny, but we had a disappointment when Alderman Illtyd Thomas's daughter got married, we tied the gate leading to Ely Farm and waited for ages but they never came back because they had their reception in town. They lived at Ely Farm for years and then Mrs Davies went there to live, their son William is still there.

Nora Coulson (née Woolven)

Ely Council School

I started school in 1908 and I remember Miss Thomas our governess. We learned to write and sound our letters in the Infants; I remember we used to dance around the maypole with pretty coloured ribbons. In the big school they were more strict. Mr Langstaff

Ely Floods 1927 showing the White Lion (left) and the Bridge Inn.

Ely Council School, around the First World War.

was our headmaster and woe betide you if you misbehaved – you had the cane and not a light stroke but one you did not want again. If we talked during lessons we had to stay in at playtime and write 'I must not talk' one hundred times. If we stayed home we had the school board man after us. He was a one armed man named Mr George and if we saw him we would run and hide because he always wanted to know what we were doing.

We always started school with a hymn and a prayer and then we went into our classes for lessons. We had no outings or games in those days and I never forgot what I learned. I remember Mr Davies we called 'Daio' behind his back, Mr Williams we called Georgie, Miss Howells we called Moppie because she had a mop of black hair and came over in the First World War from Belgium. Miss Phillips was very strict and if she caught you talking she would hit you on the head with a thimble, which she always wore. Miss Truelove was lovely.

Nora Coulson (née Woolven)

Ely Village

My memories of Ely village are happy ones. We were a busy village with a busy railway station and coal yard. We also had three breweries – Crosswells, Ely and Chivers Jam and Pickle factory - and three public houses – White Lion, the Bridge and the Red Lion. There was also a paint works and a quarry depot belonging to the Osmonds. It included a blacksmiths and carpenters shop and stables for about twenty horses as well as their tipcarts. Osmonds had a quarry in Twyn-y-Odin near Wenvoe. As well as the horses they had four steam wagons. When I was seventeen I was driving one of them.

Ed Woolven

Charabanc outings

Where Billy Davies (W.T. Davies' Transport) now has his works we used to have a fair with

Steam engine near Wenvoe, 1910.

roundabouts and swings – it caused great excitement. We had a Mr Morris who had a charabanc and we used to go on outings; he kept it in the little lane between the launderette and the taxi office in Mill Road.

Nora Coulson (née Woolven)

The races

The racecourse in my time had hansom cabs and horse and traps. The first motor taxi that turned up frightened the horses!

Ed Woolven

Ely farms

We were surrounded by four farms - Red House, Ely, Green and Sweldon - and Mill Road ended at number 100. From there it was an old lane leading to the Pumping Station. Then we had Ely Paper Mills, which employed a good many of our men. We also had two brick works; one at the foot of Caerau hill and another at the end of a lane which is now Amroth Road. Going west Ely ended by the old Highmead House owned by Ivor Vachell and of course the old round toll house which would be a bit up from the Amroth Road and Cowbridge Road junction. We had a good many rose gardens and nurseries; Treseders, Hills, Slocombes and Palmers.

Ed Woolven

Lloyd Williams

We hear a lot about Ivor Novello who was a wonderful person but no one seems to remember his companion and secretary who lived near the White Lion Hotel in a small cottage, now a betting shop in Ely. He was a brilliant pianist and I can remember how he used to open his window and play to our delight. That was about in 1912. Ivor always

Ely Farm, 1980.

used to call him 'Lloydy'. His name was Lloyd Williams.

Ed Woolven

Edwards bakery

The original house, before it became the West End Social Club, was built and a bakery started by my wife's father and uncle, Alf and Frank Edwards, just before the First World War. They had quite a number of horse and carts delivering bread to the city.

Jim Halloway

Mother's meeting outing

This year our members were enlarged by the addition of many whom Mrs Hill wished to invite with us to her lovely house on the Mendip Hills. We started at 8.30 a.m. from Ely to the Pier Head by brake and then by steamer to Weston and then again by brake for a nine mile drive to the village of Langford where we got out. In this village are Mr Vernon Hill's Nursery Gardens which we were invited to look round and then we climbed up to Mendip Lodge where we all sat down to a sumptuous repast about 2 p.m. (About fifty-four in number). After dinner we went up still higher to the Mendips and feasted our eyes with the glorious views of the Channel and the Welsh Hills and our lungs with the salubrious air. We came down again and looked all round the gardens at the sweet peas, the verbacious and alpine plans too numerous to mention here and the roses. After a good tea and saying goodbye and giving our hearty thanks to Mr and Mrs Hill we mounted our brakes and came home. We were highly favoured with one of the finest days this summer of which we had very few indeed.

Recollections of a Mother's Meeting outing in the Caerau with Ely Parish Magazine, September 1912

Lloyd Williams's house (next to 'Ty Trelai' and the White Lion, photographed on 12 May 2002) is now a William Hill betting shop.

Caerau with Ely Mothers Union.

New Ely Bridge

The Lord Mayor of Cardiff and the Chairman of the Glamorgan County Council will open our new Ely Bridge on Friday 16 June. The time will probably be about 2 p.m. On this occasion the Lord Mayor has kindly consented to present to Mr Edward A. Sydenham a certificate from the Royal Humane Society, as a reward for having, on 23 March 1911, gone to the rescue of a child who was in imminent danger of drowning in the river at Ely Bridge, and whose life he gallantly saved.

Our new bridge has been opened by the Lord Myor of Cardiff and the Chairman of the County Council, Mr Blandy Jenkins. There was very few Ely people present at the function, and it seemed almost as if it did not concern them, but nearly the whole of the juvenile population were there, so much so as to call forth a remark on the subject from the Lord Mayor.

The water has again risen to a high mark finding its way into some of the houses in Mill Road and this has happened in August and after our new bridge has been completed. I fear the new bridge is not high enough by some eighteen inches.

Story by the Revd D.H. Francis in the Caerau-with-Ely Parish Magazine, June and July 1911 and September 1912

Christmas tree at Caerau

On 30 December 1911 the children of the Caerau church Sunday school were entertained by the kind hospitality of Mr and Mrs Vivian at tea and a Christmas tree in the big kitchen kindly lent by Mr and Mrs Rolles. While the tables were being cleared after the tea the young people clustered round a gramophone in the adjoining parlour and listened to the music with manifest delight. Meanwhile a pretty Christmas tree was being lighted up in the kitchen and every one received some suitable souvenir. After this, in the presence of the parents, the prizes were

A view of the new bridge being built from Riverside Terrace 1910/11. Station Terrace and Crosswells Brewery can be seen to the right with Chivers on the left.

distributed by the Revd J.H. Du Boulay, to those who by their regular attendance, diligence in learning, and good behaviour had earned them. It was a most enjoyable treat and the children gave hearty cheers and thanks to their kind entertainers.

Revd J.H. Du Boulay

Vachell's and Highmead House

The old man who lived in Highmead, the big house, was Mr Vachell, a solicitor. When we lived in Caerau we kept chickens, everybody did. Every Saturday morning my mother got the basket ready and my sister and I used to take two dozen eggs down the lane to Mr Vachell. If Mr Vachell saw us going up the lane, and in the end we got very knowing and made sure he did see us, he always gave us a shilling each. So we had two shillings each for the eggs and a shilling each for pocket money. We kids thought he was very nice.

Highmead was the first place I saw anybody with a fur coat. We went up there one Saturday morning and saw this lovely lady; I think it was his niece. You don't see the coats now. She had a grey squirrel coat on. I didn't know what it was but my mother told me afterwards. She was well up on clothes. And a beautiful purple frock underneath.

Mrs Strong

Highmead House

When I was twelve I can remember delivering the Western Mail and the South Wales Daily News to Highmead House. The house was owned by Ivor Vachell, a solicitor, who had a brother who was a doctor. The house was later owned by Edgar Edwards.

Ed Woolven

The Vivian family – Brenda, Lesley and Gilbert.

Below: The Vivian sisters.

In the grounds of Highmead House.

Golf at Highmead

Highmead had one drive with thick chestnut trees in and the other was a private drive and we wondered what he was doing. Later on I knew there was a big pampas grass in the middle of the lawn. You could not see it from the road because it was all enclosed in a big white wall and he had a net. He was practising putting and chipping! I used to stand and watch of course, I had never seen golf or heard anything of it at all but that was the first time. Then I played golf for forty years after that! When I went back I asked my mother; 'what's he doing, he had a sort of stick and he was hitting a ball with a stick into a net'. That's called golf she said.

Mrs Strong

Nuts at Christmas

My father later went to Highmead as a gardener. He knew a lot about flowers; he was a countryman. They had there a plantation of nuts, big hazelnuts, and before Christmas he would bring some of the nuts home. They used to bury them in the garden in a couple of big pots, cover them and put them well down in the damp earth. They were wonderful at Christmas time.

Mrs Strong

Harvest at St Mary's

My father was also churchwarden at Caerau and at Harvest, which was always held on a

Thursday evening I used to get a bunch of grapes from the vinery in Highmead. They grew everything. The grapes were hung over the archway by the altar. It was his donation to Caerau. It was all very cosy.

Mrs Strong

Sewing at school lunchtime

In Caerau Lane, right at the beginning, on the left is a building, a red brick house built by Mr Morgan who had a market garden on the left-hand side. On the right hand side two houses; a woman I went to school with lived there. She went to live there after she got married and I think she died there. She was very clever. There was nobody in her family who did anything like it but at playtime in Ely school we had nobody to supervise us at dinnertime. We were twelve – fourteen children coming down from Caerau every day to school. Nobody to supervise at dinnertime but some of the teachers stayed in for lunch and the staff room was upstairs. After they had made their tea at lunchtime one of us used to go up with a brown tea pot and they would put boiling water in for us and we would have tea in one of the class rooms.

Miss Peach was very fond of sewing and when she had any pocket money she bought patterns in a little shop on the corner of the main road. And she taught us how to use patterns to make things and there was a corner in the playground that nobody ever went in to and we 'dinner girls' and the boys sometimes used to go in there and she would teach us to sew. We used to sew the paper up because we didn't have any material. That girl ended up in a shop in the High Street Cardiff in a wonderful classy shop called 'Anthonies'. She was head seamstress with no training. The Peaches were the people who supplied the milk to the village. They had a farm.

Mrs Strong

St Mary's church, Caerau, 1980.

Hancocks Hill

There was nothing in Caerau village then at all, just the one straight road and it went right round and up the hill to the church. There was nothing off the road at all. We walked to school every day when it was dark in the morning and came home in the dark at night. In the summer we cut across some fields, past the workhouse, further up some high red brick wall, what we used to call the diphtheria, scarlet fever and typhoid hospital. We used to go up the side there and across some market gardens. Where the traffic lights are on the little hill we called Hancocks Hill.

They built one house there, a red brick house, the only detached house there and that was built by Hancocks. We used to go right across his gardens, through a field, which we called the nine acres and then we came into what we called Watery Lane and then we were in Caerau. That is if it was a fine day. Mr Hancock lost lots of rhubarb and peas; in the end he got very wise and never planted anything near the right of way.

Mrs Strong

Hancocks House (Highmead Villa) on Cowbridge Road.

Caerau Isolation Hospital and Caerau House

The Isolation Hospital was over towards Cwrt-yr-Ala. Some people by the name of Hill or Allen lived there and we could go to see that place from Caerau church.

Mrs Allen lived there before it was an Isolation Hospital. She used to come to church through a little wood. The wood had the most beautiful daffodils of all kinds and we never touched one. My father killed a snake there once. I had never seen a snake and my father knew it. He got two pieces of wood with planks on top and hung the snake there for my sister and me to inspect it.

Mrs Strong

Working at Rookwood

My father was the eldest of ten children and had the land all the way down from Caerau church. At least they rented it; the farmhouse was theirs, from Colonel Hill who used to live at what is now Rookwood Hospital. My father when he was fourteen went to lodge in Llandaff and that is where he started his gardening. Colonel Hill was very strict apparently. He took my father on. My father was late one day – he arrived at five past six in the morning instead of six – and he had to appear before Colonel Hill who told him if he was late once more he would get his father out of the farm in Caerau.

Mrs Strong

Caerau Isolation Hospital.

Caerau House, 1904.

Caerau Village

We lived in Caerau. My father was the gardener in a big house in Caerau. Captain Brain, who lived at Cwrt-yr-Ala, was the churchwarden of St David's where my father was for years and years. All round the back of Ely Council school, where I started school, were allotments. No houses except for two in front of the school where the caretaker lived, Mr Bell. There was a little shop on the corner nothing else. I used to walk to school every day from Caerau, Caerau village - it was all country down the lane with banks on the side and hedges on top and mud on the floor in winter.

We had no communication between Caerau and Ely. We had a grocer coming once a fortnight to the village and he lived in Victoria Park. He used to come and get the order and bring the last one. We had a bread man twice a week and a man used to come with the pig feed. It was the highlight of our day as we always used to have a ride to the end of the village on the cart. Nobody had a bicycle.

Everybody in the village knew everybody else. I remember when I was very little that Mrs Peach was going to have a baby. You just whispered it; I didn't know she was going to have a baby. My mother asked my father for some gold sovereigns. Apparently she was very ill and they had to get a specialist out from town. He came but he would not go upstairs to see Mrs Peach until unless there were twelve gold sovereigns on the table. There was a little hunt round the village then; the Peaches had money but you didn't keep it around. My mother had about five spare, at least they weren't spare but everybody helped everybody. When pig-killing day came everybody had something off the pig. It was the only day in the year my sister and I were allowed to stay home from school. Our pig was killed in the garden.

Mrs Strong

Nurse Willis

When I was little I put my finger in a wringer. I wasn't four but from this women's garden I could see the children, including my sister who was two years older than me, coming home from school. You could see from Mrs John's garden them coming in to the village. I was then allowed to run down and meet my sister. I was down Mrs Johns garden one day, there was no washing machines then. She had a wooden tub in the garden and a wringer screwed on the side. I had never seen a

Vi Peach.

wringer before. The cogs were going round and what did I do? I put my finger in. I could not understand that the cogs were going both ways in between. It smashed my finger. We had no nurse or anything in the village but down in Ely there was Nurse Willis, she was wonderful.

My father was driving the boss into the station to catch the train – not driving by car but by pony and trap. He called in to ask her if she could spare some time to come up to Caerau. Every other morning she would come, I would sit on the table, and she would bind my finger up. It went on for years. Nurse Willis lived in a house attached to the White Lion pub. During the time I was in Herbert Thompson the poorer children had breakfast there too and Nurse Willis had her front table with benches round. We teachers had to write out all the tickets – white ones for breakfast and green ones for lunch. You can imagine we had a month's holiday and had to write all these blessed tickets out.

Mrs Strong

Penylan Farm

Penylan farm on the top was where the David's lived. They had two or three boys and one girl. The girls were Sunday school teachers.

Mrs Strong

St David's Hall

Councillor Moore lived with his brother Cliff. He was a very active councillor. He used to come over and we would have lovely dances in St David's Hall. Our social life revolved around that hall. Marvellous times there. Where the Chinese take away is now was a very famous flower and vegetable shop owned by Palmers market garden.

Mrs Strong

Vicar Marsden's induction

Vicar Marsden, I remember his induction in Caerau. My father shot a pheasant. We had oil lamps, little red oil lamps in St Mary's and my mother for the induction put out our dresses and brown straw hats. My mother put two pheasant's feathers in each hat. We always sat in the same pew in Caerau and all we did during the service was watch the reflection from the lamp casting a shadow on ourselves and on to the wall. My mother said what a nice sermon it was but my sister and I just looked at each other, as we didn't know anything about it at all!

Mrs Strong

Money

We didn't have any money, we had no pocket money but then we had nowhere to spend it. There was not a shop in Caerau. When Mr Vachell gave us a shilling each we never kept it, we didn't think it was ours. We gave it to mother.

My first job as a teacher was ten shillings a week. I never opened the envelope.

Mrs Strong

First Bricks from Caerau

I remember the first cartload of bricks that left the Caerau brickworks. We were horrified. We didn't like that at all because it meant the roads were not tidily muddy as they always had been for us to walk on.

Mrs Strong

Taking the eleven plus

We lived out of the borough as far as Cardiff was concerned to sit the eleven plus and so we

St David's Hall with Millbank (Ely Council school) in the background, 10 May 2002.

could either go to Penarth County which my mother could not afford to send us as there were no grants or go to Howells school. It was nearer so I went for the day from Lansdowne Road. We had transferred there from Ely because mother could see that Mr Longstaff, who was the head teacher when she went to see him about us sitting the eleven plus because my sister was ready now, had said 'No I never send any children in for the eleven plus because I don't believe in having nobody with any brains at the top of the school'. So my mother said; 'that's no good, we are going to have two teachers here if it's the last thing I do'. So she went down to Lansdowne school and asked the head there and it was too late for my sister to take the exam to go to Canton Sec. So the head teacher there, Miss Abbott, gave my sister a little exam on her own and she passed and she went. I was two years younger so I had to go and sit for Howells school. When it came time for me to sit the eleven plus my mother had seen an advert in the paper for a garage in Roath. She didn't even know where Roath was. We didn't have a car but she would be paying eight shillings a week rates into Cardiff and that is what enabled me to go to a high school in Cardiff.

Mrs Strong

Coming home from Cwrt-yr-Ala

Ernest Rose was from Caerau and he was killed in the war. I remember him coming into church in Caerau, he was fair, and I thought if ever I have a husband I would like him to look like that. I was only little. There was a family of Johns, four boys, they all were in the war and came back safely. Their mother used to work in Cwrt-yr-Ala and did housework. One night she didn't come back at all and everybody was in a terrible state. The next morning the dear old thing had fallen over a ditch coming from Cwrt-yr-Ala. She was taking a short cut and she fell and broke her leg. Now that really was news in the village.

The Thorne Family who owned the brickworks in Caerau, known also as the West End Brickworks.

The village was self-sufficient. My father insisted on always having a black pig in the sty, a couple of hives of bees and a lovely garden.

Mrs Strong

Ely United

When Ely was a village before there were council houses there was a senior football team called Ely United. They had great success. They played on a field near the racecourse.

Mr Hopkins

Dust in your eyes

When you used to go to Barry years ago in a charabanc you would have all dust in your eyes.

Mr Hopkins

Cwrt-yr-Ala House, Michaelston le-Pit in the 1920s and which is situated about two miles from Caerau. The Italinate villa, seen here, was replaced in 1940.

3 First World War and the Depression

Missionaries in Caerau and Ely

We were more interested in missionaries then; they used to come once a year and set up their shows in St David's Hall. When we lived in Caerau my sister played the piano. A missionary, when I was quite small, came to Caerau and we were the only ones who had a piano and they asked if they could come and take a service there every night for the week. Everybody in the village came and every night we would have hymns and this fellow would talk nicely to every body. There was one thing we used to sing, can you stand me singing it, it's very short:

'Are you right, Are you right for the mansion bright
Have you got your ticket, are the signals right
For you never know when the train may go
Get ready, get ready tonight'

Course it wasn't a bit like a church hymn so we all learnt it. We thought it was marvellous. That must have been in about 1915. The missionaries told us all about the poor life the Indians and the Africans had. It frightened us to death half the time. Another lot of missionaries used to come to St David's.

Mrs Strong

Old Ely

I was born at No. 17 Windsor Terrace, that's the row of houses between Mill Road and Colin Way on Cowbridge Road. Colin Way used to be called Paget Street but when the Ely Riverside Estate was built between 1936/37 by Mr Regan he changed the name from Paget to Colin Way after his son. I think it was the only street in Cardiff without a house in it. I was born in 1917 before a council house was built and moved to Clarke Street in 1920 – one of only three streets in Ely; Clarke Street, Robert Street, and the now gone Paget Street I went to Ely Council school, with the building of the Cardiff Council Estate, infants were sent across the road to St David's Hall with screens dividing up the classes.

When I was nine or ten I can remember them altering the course of the river at the Paper Mill end by putting a dam across to control the flood water. The house in Windsor Terrace had big front gardens then. Ely station was very active, racehorses would arrive by train be walked to the back of the White Lion, where the racecourse stables were. There were also overflow stables at Col. Llewellyn's at the Court.

At the back of the White Lion there was a tin shed, some thirty foot long, that belonged to Nurse Willis the local midwife, she was a bit deaf.

Mr H.L. Hall

Mr Greatrex was a jockey in Worcestershire and after being injured moved to Newport and then Ely.

Ely racecourse

My father was grounds man at Ely racecourse in 1914 - I was ten - and he was there for lots of the meetings and we used to thoroughly enjoy it. We would go up on the tump by St Mary's and watch the races.

Mrs Strong

First World War

The First World War had no impression on us at all as children in Caerau. My father had a marvellous allotment and in fact when the baker used to come we used to change bread and sugar for potatoes and other veg. It was a wonderful spirit of exchanging. I remember my mother had a big canister of tea, that was all she stored, and father used to say to her as long as you can get a cup of tea you don't trouble what you eat do you? And she said no

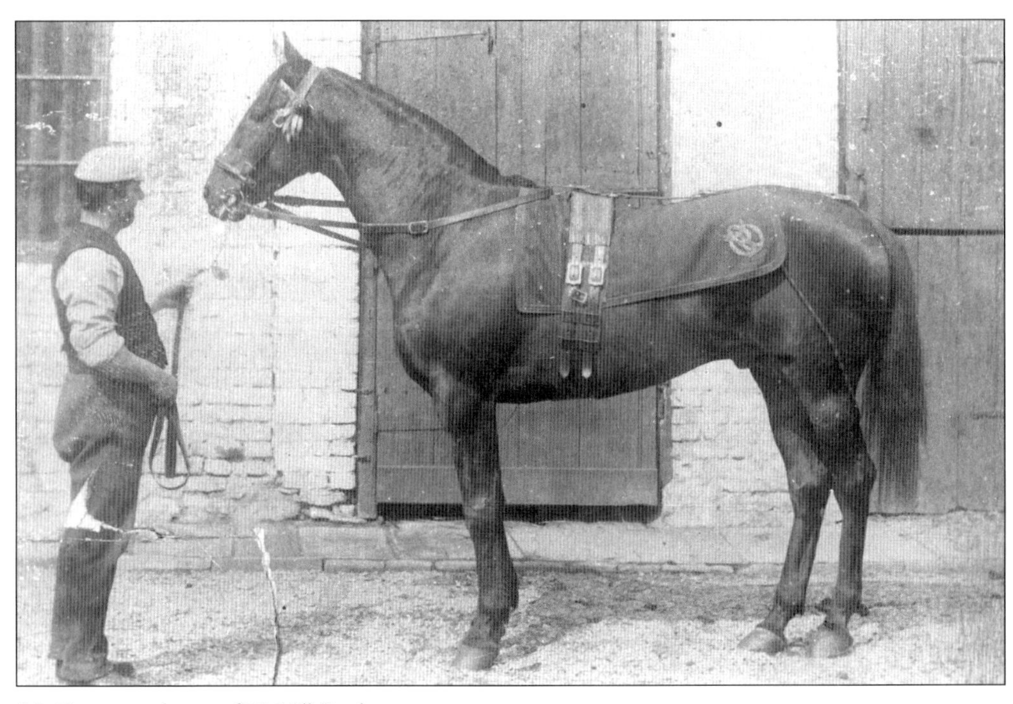

Mr Greatrex at the rear of 70 Mill Road.

I don't. You could get nothing but we had eggs from our chickens.

Mrs Strong

Ely Brewery

When peace came I was discharged early because my father had died leaving my mother with six children. I immediately went back to the brewery to work in the washhouse, which could be a very cold job in winter. If the wooden barrels were smelly the old wax lining had to be steamed out and it was then recoated with fresh wax.

Shortly after this I went over to transport using old coal fired Leylands, steel wheeled 'steamers' capable of pulling heavy loads but they were very slow. They went at a maximum of five miles per hour and were very popular then for heavy jobs. You weren't allowed to put coal on in the main streets of towns – the police would book you if they saw smoke or sparks. The steamers took a certain number of barrels and then there was a trailer that took twelve more barrels. It would take a five-ton lorry three trips to shift the amount a steamer could move in one. We went as far as Porth, Pontypridd and Port Talbot.

Because the steamers were slow we often found that in winter, especially when there was a night frost, that you could not make the return journey. We then had to phone the brewery who would say it was ok to stay the night and tell us what pub to go to for a meal. We used to have to stay with the steamer all night keeping warm from the boiler fire. In those days eight out of ten pubs in the valleys belonged to Ely Brewery and were easily recognised by their blue and white paintwork.

One of my favourite runs was to the 'Royal' on the seafront at Port Talbot. If the tide was in the cellar would be under two foot of water so there used to be a man down there in top boots. When we had unloaded and loaded up the empties the landlord would sign the book and we would go round to the kitchen for a lovely meal. One frosty night we were climbing slowly up a hill when one of the men, Ernie Hooper jumped off and ran along side. Soon the steamer picked up speed at the top of the hill and he was left behind. He had to walk all the way back to Cardiff.

Ernest Strong

Ely Brewery beer bottle, 1920s.

St Clare's Roman Catholic church, in Mill Road, June 1981.

The Irish in Ely

It seemed like the Irish community settled down in Ely here in Mill Road. A lot of Irish were down there. The Hurleys, the Caseys and the Murphys. They didn't have a church in Ely so they used to go to St Mary's in Kings Road in Canton for mass. I think sometimes they used to have mass in Ely Lodge. The Hurleys were the coal merchants; there had two brothers; Maurice and Andrew.

Mr Sparkes

Homes fit for heroes

My earliest memories are of Temperance Town, a part of Cardiff that has long since changed out of all recognition and where I lived until I was about four years old. We lived at 25 Park Street, the street still exists but all the houses have gone. My grandmother, my father's mother, lived with us and was a very stern Victorian Lady, I think we were all frightened of her and afraid to talk in front of her until she spoke to us. My father, Stanley Steadman, had fought in the First World War, lying about his age to join up and being sent to the Western Front. In France he won the Military Medal and Bar but he would never talk about his exploits, at least not to us. We found out from my mother that it was for raiding enemy trenches and capturing German soldiers. I remember people saying that Lloyd George had promised that there would be 'Homes fit for heroes' after the war and I suppose that was why council houses were built in Ely. He left the Army as a sergeant and joined the Police as a sergeant, this was before I was born but I remember him telling me about how he patrolled Tiger Bay in pairs because it was such a tough place with fights breaking out all over the place caused mainly by drunken seaman of almost every nationality you could think of.

At the time we lived in Park Street my father was working for Dunlop who had a tyre depot at the end of the street, the Army Barracks was opposite with the General Post Office alongside. My mother would sit me and my sister Sheila on the step outside the house and tell us not to move – Sheila would listen and not move an inch but I would run off to the nearby river Taff and watch boys fishing for eels off the muddy banks of the river from Wood Street bridge. Many times the nuns from nearby St Dyfrig's church, now the site of the Cardiff Buses office block, would bring me home full of mud and despite being told off I would still go back! I remember being told that all the houses in Temperance Town were coming down and we had to move, which we did, at first to Grangetown, from which we could walk to Penarth and its beach through the old tunnel, and then to Ely.

My mother broke her heart because it seemed so far from the centre of Cardiff, she felt it was like being sent abroad because Ely was so far out! My mother had worked in St Mary Street, at the Griffin pub – now demolished. My grandmother didn't come with us, instead going to live with my Uncle Tom in Ninian Park Road. We were given a new council house; No. 1 Marcross Road, which had lots of steps going up to it and a garden that was a mess. My father soon sorted the garden out being a keen gardener who won lots of prizes at vegetable and flower shows. I went to Hywel Dda and Windsor Clive schools and on leaving school at fourteen I started work in Fanbury's Dress and Fur Shop where I had to wear a black dress with a white collar, my mother hoped it would make a lady out of me! I hated every minute there and left to work in Schmitt & Son's laundry in Tudor Lane, this was run by Germans, who as bosses were wonderful. The laundry was bombed during the war, I went to work as normal one day and the building was completely gone and I never knew what happened to the owners. We had an air raid shelter in our back garden where we spent many nights, our neighbours joining us – one time I can remember going down to the shelter with measles with everybody ending up catching it!

Doreen Jones (née Steadman)

Doreen and Catherine Steadman in Temperance Town, before their move to Ely.

Stanley, Doreen and Sheila Steadman outside their house in Marcross Road, early 1930s.

Life on the Estate

There were no new homes here whatsoever, only Plymouthwood Road. It was all fields with farms and all here. It was really lovely like living in the country. No roads they hadn't been made, no lights or lamps. We had gas in the house, we didn't have any electric only gas mantles. You could have a life. We used to go picking blackberries, just behind our house. You had the freedom of the fields and if you wanted to go and camp out you could. Well we used to take our tents and we almost lived up in Plymouth Woods more or less. We'd take a bottle of water. We didn't take food we couldn't afford it. We were all poor. Maybe we would pick the pears off the trees and if we were lucky take some bread and cheese.

The river was a bit treacherous. I never went in the river. We used to walk up the 'rusty line' – the old railway – we weren't supposed to but we did until we got caught. Frank Road was all fields. There was different flowers there – dog roses, daisies, cowslips, bluebells as well as blackberries and chestnuts.

Mr Winters was the village policeman. He came at the same time as us. He lived in Plymouthwood Road. There was five wooden houses – three one side and two the other. There were steel houses in Caerau Square.

Mr and Mrs Page

The Parish

I lived in the last but one house after the Western Cemetery near the house of Colonel Llewellyn. As kids we used to perform a mock racecourse. When I was twelve or thirteen we would walk the horses. Fields were full of primroses, bluebells and rabbits. It's now a playing field.

Highmead had an Annual Fair. Bon Marche was the bus terminal we had to walk from there to Green Farm Road, which was known as No. 81 Road before that Cemetery Road. Two brothers name Coles lived in High Field. Cardiff Villa played in a field opposite the Dusty Forge near by Cardiff University had playing fields. Sweldon Farm was the old

An early view of Loughers bacon factory in Norbury Road.

farmhouse that was gutted in a tragic fire. Most farms were smallholdings. Cardiff University had an experimental growing area where the Jewish cemetery is now. Opposite on a new road was Thorne's Brickyard. Ely was a beautiful place.

Mill Road had wooden houses we used to say 'going up the walla'. They were called after a Norwegian Builder called Walla. Sadly some of the houses caught fire and two or three children were killed. Behind the houses was Treseders Nursery, it was a vast area. Behind the Avenue Cinema was Edwards Bakery where we queued up to buy stale bread during the depression.

Ely Cattle Market – Loughers would sell pork bones to make stew out of it. One man who worked there was a real character; he had a twisted withered leg for which he had a crutch made with a step in it to rest his leg. During the depression his father had two shillings and attended the labour school at the top of Bute Road.

The Drope was a mass of smallholdings, some of the farmers were Dawsons and Casey's. We would muck out the cattle for a sack of spuds. Down the Docks I remember Neale & West's trawlers docking opposite the Norwegian Church. At the top of Jackson Road was the old Rec, a swimming pool was started there with a deep and shallow end but it was never finished. There were playing fields and unemployed men would play pitch and toss. Ely was the border between the Glamorgan and Cardiff Constabulary, Inspector Hutchins was the local Inspector, if you did anything wrong he would go and see your father who would give you a belt. Cyntwell was a village now its just part of Ely. Jack Peterson opened the Culverhouse Cross pub, Charlie Fox had owned the Caerau Arms, which is now a house next door to the pub.

On the parish before you could receive any money from the 'parish' you had to sell all your luxuries otherwise when the word goes around that the parish man was coming round and you passed your goods over the fence for your neighbour to look after.

Mr H. Watkins

An internal view of Loughers factory in the 1920s.

Ely barbers in 1927

In 1927 I put up a sign saying 'Harry's coming – Harry's here' above a small shop in Wilson Road. I was the son of a barber and I went on to run the Wilson Road shop for forty years when my son Ted took over.

When I first came to Ely there were only two other shops in the road; Morris the grocer and Doddingtons the post office. Howells used to run the farm at the back of Redhouse clinic and they used it for keeping their horses and carts. Where Windsor Clive now stands I used to take my Sunday papers to read. It was a field then.

The normal work day for me was 8 a.m. to 9 p.m. and the charge for a haircut was 4d for a working man and 3d for the men who were unemployed providing they showed the yellow card which signified that they were on the dole. Children had their hair cut for 2d and this included a sweet. Mothers made sure that the boy's hair was cut as short as possible and on one occasion an irate mother brought her son back because it had not been cut short enough. She said, 'How do you expect me to be able to afford another 2d before six months has passed'. Men would borrow one another's bicycles to cycle down to Splott where the milk at John Bull Stores was half a penny cheaper. When the depression came spirits were low but one day even I was surprised when one of my regulars came in looking extra glum. He said 'Things look black today Harry'. I said why and he said; 'Well it looks like we may be losing our colonies' It seemed strange to me that somebody was so affected by the loss of a colony when most people had problems just to eat.

One Saturday afternoon I noticed a man waiting for a hair-cut and letting everyone else go before him. At the end of the afternoon I said well, you are the last one so it's got to be your turn. Looking a bit sheepish he told me he hadn't come in for a haircut but to listen to the radio! They cost 2/6d a week then and not many families could afford to have one.

Barbers on Sundays always went to the houses of sick men to shave them and cut their hair free. No barber worth his salt would refuse an offer to visit a sick man on a Sunday. Life was hard in those days but people were always ready to help each other. Ely is a great place to live, the people are wonderful. No swank just good working class people.

Harry Jennings

The dole

In 1923 we were on the means test. They wanted you to sell a little table or a bit of furniture. My husband used to do a bit of photography and he took a photo of a tree over the field that had been struck by lightning. It was in the paper and he got eighteen shillings for it. They stopped him money. I was hard up and put in for money. They came to the house and said sell your saucepans. I said I need them to cook. He said you don't need them all! Sell your bedding. That's what I had to do. After that I said I would never ask for a thing off the social. And if you left your rent that was terrible. It was five shillings a week.

Mr and Mrs Page

Going to school in Ely and Wenvoe

Mr Langstaff the headteacher of Ely Council school seemed an old man and wore a skullcap. He only taught when a teacher was missing. If you missed school for one or two days you would have a school inspector coming to your house. When you went back they expected a note from your parents. The place I lived was in the row of cottages on the way to Barry (now called Brooklands Terrace) near

Wenvoe school and School House, 1934. Morriss's Stores van can be seen in the background.

Culverhouse Cross. They were built for the men who built the railway tunnel, which goes from the Drope and comes out on the way to Wenvoe. It was the Valley line. The breather is still there. The cottages were in a field and the little tower, when a train went through the smoke came out because they were steam then. Anyway I used to walk from there to school in Ely - there was no school dinners then. I went there because my parents wanted me to go there because they knew some families associated with the school. I could have gone to Wenvoe or St Georges but it made no difference, I would have had to walk.

When Ely became part of the city of Cardiff I had to go to Wenvoe. There was a big difference. I was about twelve and a half to thirteen by then and I was far above the others in the way of education. There was only two teachers there. Mr Rex, who was the headmaster, and his wife. He looked after the seniors and she the juniors. The standard was not so high and you had to attend church on religious days, as it was a church school. Occasionally Mrs Jenner's nephew; Mr Thompson, would have a shoot and the school kids had to volunteer to go beating.

Mr W. George

School assembly

In Herbert Thompson after Miss Williams we had a head teacher Ruth Parry, who was very musical. She would have a hall full of kids and she would sit down and sing humorous songs to them and play the piano. How things have changed since I was in Ely school. When you went into the hall every morning on the floor there was brass nails put at distances in a line. We had to stand on those nails and I was only four and if you fell off a nail you got a smack. All this took place during the prayers. We had to do this for twenty minutes with both feet together. That's how we had the lines.

Mrs Strong

Victoria Park postcard.

Victoria Park

In Victoria Park there was all the animals you could think of in a cage - parrots, budgies, peacocks, monkeys, and tortoises but Billy the Seal was the main attraction. There were two seals to begin with but one died. It was a big outing going down there. The gardens were beautiful too.

We couldn't go to school when we had the 1927 floods. We used to watch the rowing boats going down taking people to Canton. That was a big flood that was. They lost a lot of animals in Victoria Park. They also had an elephant and a camel. On certain days they'd take the people round the park for a ride. It cost about a penny. People came from everywhere to go to the park.

Mr and Mrs Page

Leaving school

I left school on the 14 June 1917 and started work in Chivers jam factory. One of the highlights of Ely Council School was on 29 May 1937 when one of their pupils, Moyna Mullet, was chosen to be Cardiff's May Queen. She was crowned by the Lord Mayor of Cardiff Alderman Herbert Hiles, MBE, JP at the New Theatre, Cardiff. She was a lovely girl and deserved the honours.

Nora Coulson (née Woolven)

From the Rhondda to Ely

My mother Elizabeth (Danny) Daniel, née Evans, was born in Blaenllechau in the Rhondda, but had moved to Tylorstown by the time I was born. I know she went through a tough time in the depression and helped out in a soup kitchen set up by the chapel in 1921. The chapel was a strong influence in the family. I can remember eating in a soup kitchen set up during the miner's strike in 1926. Like most men in the Rhondda, my father was a miner and worked at the nearby Rhondda No. 8 pit. He was to die of the miners disease, silicosis, in 1939. My mother

Soup Kitchen in Tylorstown during the strike 1921. Elizabeth (Danny) Daniel is fifth from the right in the middle row.

never remarried and I was to move away to find work – at first to London to work in service and later to train as a nurse in St Giles, Camberwell. Owing to the bombing, doodlebugs and rockets, I finished my training at a hospital in Dartford, Kent and it was there that I met my future husband Tom Cumner. I returned to Cardiff at the end of the war, where I got married and lived with my mother in rooms in Newport Road. Four years later, with my husband, two children and my mother we moved to our first council house in Stanway Road, Ely.

Muriel Cumner (née Daniel)

From Canton to Ely

I moved to Ely when I was eight years old - that was in 1924 and we lived at 45 Ty Coch Road. We came from Canton, 11 Glamorgan Street, and before that Romilly Road West where I and my eldest brother Keddie – christened Kedwyn Hathaway was born. I remember going to old Ely school and sometimes we would have to go across the road to classes in St David's Hall, I nearly didn't live to move to Herbert Thomson school when it opened as one day I ran out of the lane – that was the short cut from old Ely school – behind a bus and straight on to the main Cowbridge Road. I almost run straight under a car but instead bounced off its front wheel and landed on the road, where I immediately picked myself up and ran across to the other side of the road as I thought another vehicle was fast approaching. When I paused to catch my breath with my friends in front of the chemist - then on the corner of Mill Road, I realised it was a steam lorry that

Chivers workers trip to Cheddar, 1920s.

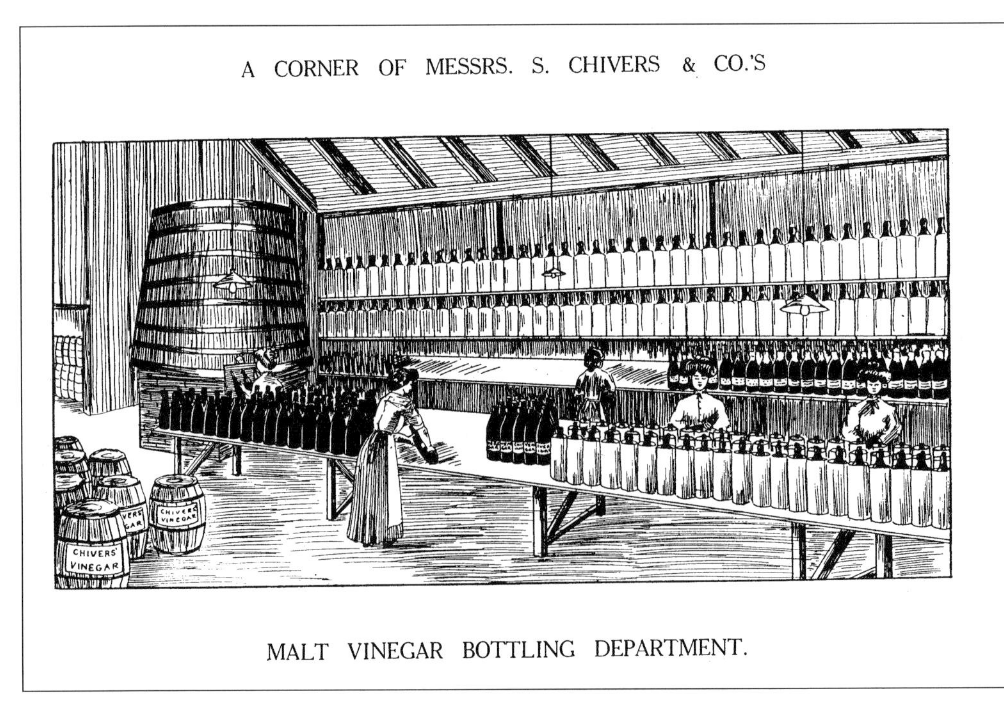

Line drawing of Chivers Malt Vinegar Bottling Department, 1918.

was still crossing the bridge! The driver of the car had braked, believing he had run over me and could not understand where I had got to, but as I just had bumps and grazes I made my way home to Ty Coch Road, I don't think I even told my parents!

Marjorie Elsie Gwendoline Macdonald (née Jones)

Changing Ely

On the site of the Regent Cinema was a cottage owned by Captain Taysome who was a retired sea captain. I remember them grinding the ceiling mortar for the Regent Cinema in a yard owned by Charles Pidgeon in Mill Road. The 'Dagear' was a right of way between Mill Road and Cowbridge Road, which is now Heol y Felin.

Ed Woolven

Unemployed in the 1930s

In the 1930s we used to have two pence and a ticket. Then you would go to the house and have a bowl of pea soup. The house was run by the Board of Guardians and relief board. Things were so bad you would go back and forth every week with your father's suit or your blanket or boots to the pawnshop. If you wanted a pair of hob nailed boots you went to the Board of Guardians and they did test work. I remember going for a food ticket, which was seven and six pence. I had it and then three days later I had to go and move all the snow off the roads with a shovel and brush. If I had not turned up for work I would not have had the ticket.

Then when I had a pair of boots I had to go down the Ely Homes. It used to be full of Home Boys. They were dressed in blue trousers, blue coat and hob nailed boots. They would be up at six in the morning, them kids, and I use to go down there and work on the garden to 'earn' my pair of boots.

My dad formed an organisation called The Unemployed, which you paid one penny a week. Some of these people if they fell on hard times and went to the dole they wouldn't give them anything. The Unemployed used to hold meetings in the 1920/30s. My dad was an old socialist of the Keir Hardie days. He used to help all the unemployed. We had the Conservatives put out here, the Communists, Labour, the Independents but not the Liberals. He fought to have the clinic built. Llewellyn Avenue was named after him. He was Thomas Llewellyn. We, The Unemployed, helped to build Pethybridge Hall. It was something to do. The first caretaker of the hall was Mr Harris. We all used to go in there for somewhere to go and they used to run a boxing club. I moved here in 1925/26 – Ty Coch Road.

Mr Llewellyn

Hardship and poverty

Times were hard. There was very little dole. If you had no money, you had no money, that was it. Quite a lot of people had boiled potatoes and oxo for Sunday dinner. A girl I used to know who was a teacher in Grangetown used to collect all the jam jars and take them down and get all the half pennies off them and give them to the children to buy some food. Men were unused to work and lived so frugally for so long that quite a few died through the strain.

People would come round and if you had a nice bit of furniture they would say, sell that. You wouldn't get anything for it. They would take their furniture upstairs and hide it under old blankets so they weren't told to sell it. Around us the poverty was terrible. Out of our whole street there would be about five men working.

Ladies over Fifties club, Pethybridge Hall

Church of the Resurrection

Memories fade with the passing of the years but I recall the laying of the foundation stone as vividly as if it took place yesterday. There was a large number of priests and people from the parishes of the Deaneries of Penarth and Cardiff present to share in our excitement and joy. The stone was laid by the Rt Hon. Lord Glanely, the donor of the church, and the dedication prayers were said by Timothy Rees, the Lord Bishop of Llandaff.

The service was choral. We had a large choir of men and boys and it grieves me now to realise that all the men of the choir are now dead.

After the service refreshments were provided for our guests and the congratulation speeches were made by Lord Glanely, the Bishop and myself.

Those were the years of the great depression when almost all men in the parish were unemployed. But the laying of the foundation stone symbolised that hope for the future still existed in the hearts of people.

Recollections of the Revd Redvers C. Evans in 1984 on the occasion of the Church of the Resurrection's fiftieth anniversary

Making do

We were never hungry. There was always something. Everybody was poor when they moved to Ely. We were all in the same position. I used to go over Loughers and get a bag of bones for a shilling to make a soup or stew. My other sister used to go down Prices and get the cuttings of the tomatoes; a big bag for a shilling. I used to get coke off the tip. When they were building Herbert Thompson school they used to tip the ashes and everything down there. We used to be down there looking for big lumps of coke; then we'd come home, well you'd do anything for your parents.

Mr and Mrs Page

Red House clinic, 4 November 2001, shortly before the building was demolished.

Ely Council school, 1928.

The laying of one of the two foundation stones at Pethybridge Hall, 1933.

The Church of the Resurrection congregation outside the Hut. The Hut became a meeting place for worship and social life before the 'Res' was built.

Loughers advertisement from the 1930s.

4 The Development of the Estate

The first shops

Phyllis Crescent (Heol Muston) used to be our shopping centre. It even had a fish and chip shop - houses were turned into shops. You had sweet shops, groceries, faggots and peas and one or two shops in Caerau Square. The first travelling shop was Morriss's travelling stores – he came with a van in the 1920s. There were a couple of blacksmiths in Ely. One was attached to a row of cottages (Bowens Row) where Jubilee Cottages are now. There was a shop on the end of the row selling papers and sweets. The fellow who owned that shop was also a chimney sweep. There was another blacksmith's up at the Dusty Forge and one down in Mill Road. They disappeared one by one.

There was Dowlings, the fish king, Walter Graham – we called him the donkey boy because he would go round with his donkey and cart selling groceries. He lived up in Stanway Road. Parsons, who came from Cathays, sold salt and vinegar.

Mr Bradley

Caerau Square

In Caerau Square we formed a committee - Mr Patreane was on with me. We used to collect the money and give it to the secretary. We collected every week.

When I came out here to live in Ely in 1922 it was all fields. Caerau Square was the first to be built; it was called Other Square. Other Square was named after Lord Glanely's son who was killed in the First World War. We didn't like the name and got it changed to Caerau Square. Phyllis Crescent and Ronald Place followed by Windsor Green and then Archer Crescent. They were the first lot of houses I saw built; St David's Hall is where I used to go. They had social evenings and I hired the hall for a social evening of Caerau Square residents.

I moved to the prefabs in 1947 after twenty-five years in Caerau Square.

Mrs Marjorie King

Do I remember Caerau Square? I'm still living there after forty-five years. I did not have a concrete house so I didn't have to move. The concrete houses were jinxed from the start; they were nice and roomy but the great fault was concrete. Even the bedroom floors were concrete – too cold in winter and too hot in summer. The tenants were a good crowd, cleaned their homes and trimmed their gardens and were most friendly.

Mrs Tompkins

Dorothy and Thelma Mcelveen outside Caerau Square in about 1930.

Dorothy Mcelveen and friend outside Caerau Square, 1930s.

Building the first houses

See, what happened in Ely is there were dozens of builders and they were building everywhere. Part of Ty Coch Road was done, part of Red House Road, Plymouthwood Road, part of Frank Road but none were completed. Matter of fact some didn't get completed until after the war. The three roads that were complete were Hiles, Howell and Elford.

Mr Bradley

Building the Estate

I worked for Addicotts and built Charteris Road. I was tea boy for five shillings a week. After making the tea I used to have to go up the scaffold and carry 300-400 bricks and five spots of pink mortar. The bricklayer would put them away before breakfast. If it was raining we used to go in the shed and sit down. You never got paid. Then I went over the paper works for two years.

Twenty men put up a street of fifty houses in six months. I remember a block of four in Pendine Road when the Clerk of the Works inspected it and the building was four inches out. They made them take it down again as it had already been blown down once by the high wind.

I built houses in Vachell Road, Gough Road, Aberthaw Road, Jubilee Cottages, Highmead Road and Fonmon Crescent. I worked on all those sites. It seemed to be as one chap was running down his contract another one would get a contract and you'd go down and see him and say I'm finishing here this week, any chance of a job. Yes, come and see me on Monday morning. This was in the 1930s. My house was built in 1928. This bit of ground, including the council yard, was Redhouse Farm.

Mr Southall

Ely housing team

My grandfather, Edwin James Wisbey, came to Ely in 1927. Originally from London, he settled first in Aberdare and then moved to Cardiff searching for work. He found work with the Corporation as a plasterer forming part of the Ely Housing Team, which was based at Redhouse Farm. He was part of the great post war drive to build, 'Homes fit for Heroes', which in Cardiff, was the building of the Ely Garden Suburb. He considered himself lucky to be allowed to rent one of the new houses in Howell Road just off the Grand Avenue. In its large garden he built an aviary where he bred budgerigars and he also grew much of his own fruit and vegetables. He kept a dog, 'Prince' which he used to take down to the duckponds at the bottom of what later became Crossways Road and the dog would swim to the nests of the moorhens that lived on the pond, collect an egg and return to my grandfather with the egg unbroken in its mouth. A welcome addition to the family diet!

Anne Gardner

Edwin James Wisbey outside his house in Howell Road, early 1930s.

Moving in to Ely

My mother paid 16s 6d a week rent for a house in Wilson Road and when we got up there the path was stones and a big garden either side. When we went there first of all the house must have been let before and the people used to keep pigeons in there. They allowed my mother a week's rent to clean the house. That was a lot of money in those days, 16s 6d, so we cleaned the house. There were no schools up there; Snowden Road and all that side was not built. There were no shops and it was all wild. When we woke up in the morning we'd find cows in the front.

Mrs E.M. Moreland

St Mary's Caerau

We attended services at Caerau church and my two sons were choirboys. The churchwarden was Mr Arthur John and the choirmaster Ron Lark. He was also the organist. I was a member of the church council and we met at St David's vicarage when the Revd Redvers Evans was vicar. I was a sidesman at the opening of St Timothy's church and played the organ when the regular organist was not there.

Jim Halloway

Fixing the cross

The Church of the Resurrection was not built when my grandparents first arrived in Ely, work beginning in 1934. As a child I was told a story about my grandfather, that he had fixed the cross in place on the top of the church. The first man to try and do so had slipped and fallen and others were reluctant to make a second attempt, but my grandfather being a plasterer was quite used to working on roofs (tiling being then part of a plasterers job), so volunteered and succeeded in fixing the cross in place.

Anne Gardner

Ely flood prevention scheme

I retired after working for forty-seven years in the workshops for Cardiff City Council. I started as a boy on 6 June 1929. I worked for them when they diverted Ely River from Ely Bridge to behind the paper mills to Leckwith. It was called Ely Flood Prevention Scheme and the engineer in charge was Mr T.J. Evans. The foreman was William Povey of Fairwater. All the work was done by men with pick and shovels, as they had no excavators or vehicles. They hired horses and two wheel tipper trucks from David Lloyd of Glamorgan Street.

Jim Halloway

Church Farm, St Mary's

My grandfather and father were born in Llandinam, Montygomeryshire. My grandfather came to work in the coalmine at Llanbradach and was in the Llanbradach Glee Society. My father, David Humphries, purchased a milk round from Alderney Diaries in Severn Road, Canton. In about 1928/29 he rented Church Farm, Caerau near the church. He had two milk rounds covering Ely, Splott, Grangetown and Canton. The milk was delivered on a horse and cart.

The farm had four bedrooms, a kitchen and hall/stairway. Attached to the house was a

The clergy and churchwardens of St David's church and the Church of the Resurrection, 1945.

diary and washhouse. The farm had fifty-eight to sixty-nine acres scattered around the area. Some of the fields were down by the Western Welsh offices. In the field on the left before you reach the church stood an old windmill, which had a pump. My grandfather had to pump for water and use to attach a leather strap around his foot and then press up and down to pump. In the same field was a ruin of a house.

Tramps used to sleep in the brickworks at night and one was called 'Pencils'. He use to buy pencils, cut them in half and charge the same price for each half as he had paid for the whole one!

I went to school in Windsor Clive and later Hywel Dda. We moved out of the farm in 1937 and moved to a farm in Pencoedcae. I was eleven at the time and had to drive a horse and cart loaded with chickens from Caerau to Pontypridd.

Mrs Frankton

The River Ely in flood. Fairfield Avenue, Victoria Park, 1927.

Ely Floods looking up Mill Road.

Land belonging to Church Farm, Caerau, photographed in 1979 before the building of the Ely Link Road.

West End Brickworks

I married my husband Thomas in 1926. At that time he was a miner and then he worked on ships before he worked on building sites.

In the early years of our marriage we lived in a cottage where five fields had to be crossed to get spring water. In those days there was a farm on the site of Amroth Road. In 1945 we moved from the cottage that was condemned to a council house in Deere Road.

Then shortly before my husband retired in 1950 he heard of a job at the brickworks, which also meant managing a smallholding. The accommodation was a pre-war Nissen Hut which had been renovated but it had no electricity or water. He took the job as caretaker and we stayed there until 1959. The hut was up Church Road and called Brickworks Bungalow. Mr Thorne was the owner then.

We kept chickens, pigs and geese on the smallholding and one Christmas we even supplied the management with a pig.

It was a hard life at the bungalow. Cooking was done on the open fire and my husband had to lay pipes himself to bring water from the works and then the water only went as far as the pig sties. In the winter the water froze which made it difficult especially when my daughter had her first child at the bungalow.

Mrs T. Way

The Regent Cinema

I went to the Regent every night. I would leave my jug at the corner shop and picked it up on the way home full of faggots and peas.

Mrs Tompkins

Ely Station

I remember when Ely Station was open. In the summer, Sundays, bank holidays and school holidays, families would crowd the station for a train to Barry. Many's the time I left the rent to go to give the kids a treat.

Mrs Tompkins

Whippet racing

I remember when the dog track was in the field, which is now Vachell Road. I won nine shillings for six pence.

Mrs Tompkins

The railway

My father was a signal linesman for the GWR and looked after crossing gates at Ely Paper Mill, Cartwright Lane, Sanatorium Road and Leckwith Road before the overhead railway

Above and below: Pigs kept on land around the old West End Brickworks.

Boys waiting on Ely Station, 1937.

bridges were built. I worked at Ely station and used it to travel to Penarth, Lavernock, Sully and Barry Island. Lougher's piggery was in Wroughton Place and there was a small gate to cross the railway to Fairwater before the footbridge was built.

Jim Halloway

Teaching in Herbert Thompson

I taught in Herbert Thompson when it first opened: there was eighteen staff and we taught all girls. I had taught in London for a few years. You know in those days you couldn't get a job even if you knew someone. Jobs were so scarce. I had a sister who was a little bit older than I was but she couldn't get a job in Cardiff. They put her name down, there was a list in City Hall, anyone could go in and see the list as it was an open invitation. You knew exactly who was in front or behind you all the time. There was never any name taken off, you were a number and moved up when the jobs became available. Of course when Herbert Thompson opened there were lots of jobs available.

When I started in Herbert Thompson it was the first school built for that generation. I left London on 31 March on Tuesday and started on Wednesday 1 April. I lived in Mill Road then. There was a Miss Williams who was very nice and very deaf. She didn't know what to do with me. There was thousands of children. I was put straight away in a room with Miss Miles, a huge room; with I don't know how many children, we had to divide them up.

It was the first time I had to really look after myself. I had been in a church school in London and everyone was so easy going and lovely. Miss Miles was very little. She took me to one side and said rather than divide the children up lets divide the lessons up. I said all right. Miss Miles said I will take reading and something else; you can take dictation and history. She landed me with all the jobs that had writing to do and I was there a fortnight before I realised what was happening. I was working until eight 'o' clock at night marking because there was about sixty compositions to mark. It was dreadful. I drew the line at that after a bit but we got on all right.

I taught sixty children in Herbert Thompson. It was the first school that was built without a hall, a long corridor and the hall was on its own like a classroom. You could go from one end of the school to the other. It used to be like Severn Road with the hall in the middle of the school. When I had a class in the hall there was Standard Seven in there – thirteen to fourteen year olds. That was as high as it went. There was nothing dividing the classes in the hall and I had Standard Two, sixty children, and in the top corner of the hall was the boy's class. Hundreds of children in the hall. The boys had the playtime slightly different to the girls. Everybody in the class could see what was going on somewhere else because our screen only came up to waist height. Every time anyone wanted to use the piano, the piano was kept in the hall, it had to be dragged out and then put back. It went on for five years that I was there. We all pulled together.

Mrs Strong

Teacher's wages

The children always knew when the wages arrived. A man used to come in a taxi with a big book and the cash. He took it into the staff

Herbert Thompson Girls school staff, 1929.

Herbert Thompson girls school staff, early 1930s.

room and you signed a big book. The children used to say, 'Here's the man with the money Miss'. Then one day somebody said he had counted up at the end to go in the Infants and he was £5 short. Would all the staff look to see if they had the correct money. When I looked at mine I had three £5 notes, a £1 note and half a crown. I shouldn't have had three but they were all stuck together. I was getting £11 two and six then.

Mrs Strong

Health

I went to Ely school. The head teacher was Langstaff. He used to wear a little black skullcap and always carried a cane. The first dentist was in Mill Road and the doctors were Desmond and then Williams. We used to pay three pence a week to the doctor. He used to come round on the bike to collect it. I use to work sixty to seventy hours a week for five shillings and then they took three pence out of that. One penny for the blind, one penny for the infirmary and a penny for something else. You had no choice, they stopped it out of your money. You could not afford the dentist so you went to Cardiff Royal Infirmary and had your tooth out under gas.

Mr Llewellyn

Ely homes

One of the fitter's mates he was in the Ely Homes as a child. He said his father was taken bad and not long after his mother was the same; there was no one to take him so they shoved them in Ely Homes, which was next door to Ely Lodge. They were separate.

Mr Southall

Ely Council football team, 1937.

Ely Council school, 1920s.

Rat Tat Ginger

For devilment the priests house just across the road in Grand Avenue we used to play rat-tat ginger on the front door. It was considered worse because it was the priest's house.

Mrs Dollah

Redhouse Farm

When the Ely council house estate was being built during the twenties and thirties, Redhouse Farm's buildings were used as a storage area for materials and machinery. Red House itself was used as living accommodation for our family. My father was the chief architect for all the houses built on the estate and was given the use of Red House in order to monitor the progress of the site.

Tony Simmonds

Guy Fawkes and rag and bones

On Guy Fawkes Night we never used to make a guy. Many a time I used to sit in a pushchair dressed up as a guy and we used to go by the Dusty Forge or the Culverhouse pub because there were no pubs this side. Gosh we used to have a lot of money. In Wilson Road there used to be an ice cream factory. At the top of Green Farm Road, round the Macdonald area, there was a rag and bone merchants. You used to take all your rags and jam jars up there and he bought them off you. His name was Bruno.

Mrs Dollah

Shopping in Ely

On Wilson Road the supermarket there used to be a young lady sitting in the cash desk and

Redhouse Farm, mid-1920s.

you used to have to pull a little wooden container. You would put the money inside the container and pull a pulley wire. The container would run all the way to the girl in the cash desk. The butter wasn't packed like it is now. It would be in big slabs and they would slice it off say half a pound and they had two wooden pats to pat it in to shape for you. Nothing was prepacked.

We used to play in the opening by Windsor Clive school; they would leave the doors open for us so if it was raining we used to go into the hall. They knew you wouldn't hurt anything in there.

Mrs Dollah

Redhouse Farm entrance gate from Red House Crescent, mid-1920s.

The races

It was absolutely heaving down there. You could always tell who had won - they came away smiling. You would see a lot more cars during the races than you would see the rest of the year. Not many people had cars in 1936/7

Racing at Ely on Tuesday 22 April 1930.

but they were all bumper-to-bumper round Pendine and Penygarn Roads.

Ladies over fifties club, Pethybridge Hall

Gardens

Mr Harris, he was something to do with the housing, he used to come round and look at your garden. He'd tell you if it wasn't tidy and said they could evict you if it wasn't cleaned up.

Ladies over fifties club, Pethybridge Hall

Working on the Estate

My father was a professional gardener and he moved in to the gardener's cottage in Caerau village. He always seemed to get the foreman's jobs but he was a devil for roaming. There were six of us in our family and we were all born in different places. Soon after we moved in my father died. It was a tied cottage so my mother had to get out of it so they gave her a house in Crossways Road – No. 22.

There seemed to be three main council builders – Addicott, Brown and Egland. They seemed to have the bulk of the contracts. If you had a good name for working when one contract was running down you would go to another boss and he would start you right away.

I worked in the local chemist on Grand Avenue for eighteen months straight after I left school. The hours were 9 a.m. to 8 p.m. Monday to Friday and nine till nine on Saturday. Even though that was the finishing time it was nothing for the boss to say deliver these medicines on the way home.

Mr Southall

The first shops

They were building all the time – Plymouthwood Crescent, Archer Road – and I thought that's it. There were no shops but

Grand Avenue, mid-1930s.

Butchery room at Loughers Bacon Factory at Ely Market, Norbury Road.

they allowed you to have shops in houses then. My mother used to have a shop. There were a couple of shops in Mill Road in the very old houses. First of all my mother had the shop in the pantry because we had a big family. She sold bread, milk and sugar. My mother in law used to sell beer – she brewed her own beer and sold it for a penny a bottle. There used to be a queue. She'd give a couple of sweets to kids if they brought the bottles back.

Mr and Mrs Page

Elections

Tom Llewellyn was a good man. He was a parish councillor. When it used to be elections there would be all the kids in Ely dressed up in green and white – Labour colours. We'd have the prams all dressed up too and we'd go round the streets singing. That's how we used to do it and it was great. 'Vote, vote for Tom Llewellyn.' He used to fight for us. He ran the Labour campaign for five or six years.

Mr and Mrs Page

Ely market

We'd go over to Ely market; it was by Loughers in Fairwater. You could buy veg and they sold pigs, cows, sheep, birds, dogs, cats and a monkey in a cage. I'd spend hours and hours over there. I had sixpence to clean out the pigsties.

Mr and Mrs Page

Scout troop at Ely Homes.

Ely Hospital Girl Guides.

Trips and fairs

We used to have street trips in a charabanc to Barry Island. That was something we used to look forward to. We would sometimes go on a coal truck. They used to have the fairground at Highmead House and also over the quarry. Dodgems, horses, roll a penny, chair planes; I used to like them but horses were my favourite.

Mr and Mrs Page

Ely homes

Ely Homes, yes they used to march all the children down in a crocodile to St David's church. The houses were all facing a green square with chestnut trees. It was nicely laid out. They demolished them all except two; one was kept as a ward and one as a training school. You went in the drive; there was a 'dogs leg' and then a big green. There was a padded room once; they were put in there for their own safety. That was brought up in the enquiry.

The ideal ratio was one to one but in those days it was about thirty to one. I have been on a ward with sixty-six patients and there would be two of us on all day. You would go in the bathroom after breakfast and you'd be there to dinnertime just bathing. Every Wednesday afternoon all those who were capable of walking there they would go round to the Regent cinema. Then on Saturday you'd take twelve to Ninian Park to watch the City. You'd walk there and back whatever the weather. There was no budget for bus fares.

It was one of the perks on race day you could stand on the fire escape and you could see the whole racecourse. Very often you'd see a loose horse galloping up here with his saddle still on and his number flapping.

The men (patients) used to wear flannelette shirts with no collars and a lot of them were made in the sewing room. They had flannelette pants with a tie waist and the stockings were made in the sowing room and they would be up above the knee like old farmer's stockings. Most of the men wore clogs with wooden soles.

They always had good food down there; the hospital had its own gardens and piggeries. They had a garden up at Sweldon where the housing estate is now and where the fire station is they had a big piece there and where Arles road is now on the left-hand side that was hospital gardens. They were self-sufficient. All the male patients who were capable of work used to work on the gardens and I must say they loved it and they would sell a lot of produce. They also used to provide the Infirmary, Llandough and Whitchurch with green vegetables.

I can remember several girls who were simply in there because they were single girls who had babies.

When they went to church the girls sat on the left and the boys on the right.

Mr and Mrs Keays

Mrs Thorne, a nurse at Ely Hospital.

On the streets of Ely

We use to play football every Saturday morning in Jackson Road. We use to play between buses - every two buses, half an hour, half time. We had to stop every quarter of an hour for a bus to come up the street.

We use to also play roller skating hockey in the street with rolled paper for a ball. We couldn't afford a real one.

Alf Cockle used to come round every Sunday as regular as clockwork and he used to sell fish. He would come up the street with this old carrier sack and I would have a look. He used to have a box on the top and if he had a box on the bottom as well he had cockles. One box meant fish only. Hake was very dear in fish shops then.

Mr Bradley

Cardiff races advertisement.

Ely racecourse

I went to Herbert Thompson school for two years and then Canton Secondary school. When I was at Canton the school sports ground was at Ely Racecourse even though it was still functioning as a racecourse. If there was a race meeting on our sports day it was cancelled so we used to go to the races by the 'back door'. We'd go up the left-hand side of where Amroth Road now is and past the Ear Nose and Throat Hospital. It was a lane called Hancock's Lane. We'd go up there and eventually come to the woods, go in the woods, along, back out and run across the course and right into the stands.

Harry Griffiths

Medical teatment

To get free medical treatment you had to belong to a Friendly society. It was very cheap. Your contributions were deducted from your pay by means of stamps. Your employers stamped your card; one for health insurance and the other for unemployment benefit. It was called the 'Lloyd George scheme' because he introduced it.

Dr Williams had his surgery up by the church on Grand Avenue. You'd go up there on a Saturday night and he dispensed his own medicines. If he thought you needed some cough mixture he'd nip into the dispensary and mix you some up in a bottle. Children had a lot more diseases then - rickets I remember.

Harry Griffiths

Councillor Flynn's shop

Councillor Flynn owned a big hardware store near where Heol y Felin meets the main road opposite the church, a bit down from that, it was a huge building with two shops in it. I think he owned the whole block. He also had a yard round in Mill Road that was full of junk and scrap. He was always on in the elections about how he was going to clean up Ely but his yard was the biggest mess. He made concrete blocks as well.

Harry Griffiths

Grand Avenue fountain

There was a wrought iron fountain at the end of Grand Avenue where the dual carriageway ends before the shops. It wasn't terribly big we used to climb on top of it as kids. It had a wrought iron canopy with four or five columns coming down, on a plinth with a couple of steps coming up to it and two cups on chains and you used to press the button and water came out.

Harry Griffiths

Herbert Thompson School song

In Herbert Thompson we had houses named after saints – David, Llewellyn, Dewi Sant and so on. The school song was:

On the confines of the city
By and round the Ely stream
Stands the school we love so dearly
Where we work and play and dream

Harry Griffiths

Caerau Arms

The building next to the Culverhouse pub used to be the Caerau Arms. What happened was that Mr Fox kept it and when they built the Culver they gave him that place.

Mr Bradley

The formation of the West End Club

The West End Club was originally the Ely

Some of the runners in the Welsh Grand National on Cardiff (Ely Racecourse) taking the water jump, Wednesday 23 April 1930.

Garden City Club. That was opened in Whitsun 1928. After about five years when the Council bought the ground the Council gave them Highmead House; it had been a nursing home prior to that, and they allowed them to use it for five years. Then they moved to Ash Cottage, Edwards the baker's house. Mr Edwards who owned the White House put in for it to be a pub or club of his own. It was his own ground. They turned him down and so he asked three blokes who used to clean the carts for him on a Sunday – that was Alf Humphrey, Ginger Russ and my father. Go and get twenty signatures and open up a club.

Mr Bradley

Electric and gas

Two lots of lighting you could put on in your house - gas light or electric. You had to put a shilling in the electric and if you didn't have a shilling you put a penny in the gas. Gas was duller than electric.

Mr Bradley

Bicycles

The traffic you had to watch then was bikes. There would be thousands of bikes coming up Lansdowne Road to Ely after finishing work. They rode six abreast.

Mr Bradley

The first policeman on the estate

Our first year was in Phyllis Crescent. The first policeman lived there and he had bars in his pantry where he would detain them while he waited to get in touch with Canton.

Mr Bradley

Phyllis Crescent (later renamed Heol Muston) in the mid-1930s.

Laying of the Herbert Thompson school foundation stone on 6 July 1925 by Mrs H.M. Thompson.

Windsor Clive School

Well Windsor Clive was a 'sunshine school' as they called it. It was the only one of its kind. The classrooms when the doors were opened had these partitions which they could put back and they were facing on to the playground. Every year they always used to be in the Seagar Cup for football and always seemed to be in the final. Windsor Clive was black and white squares. The teachers was Mr James, Mr John, Dickie Dyer (the Head) who was a good friend of George Thomas, Mr Gray who lived in Canton and Mr Chris Evans, the art master

Mr Bradley

Walks from school

Children in Herbert Thompson school for an afternoon out walked through St Fagans. They would never pick a primrose or daffodil. We used to take forty to fifty kids with perhaps a packet of biscuits. They were marvellous kids even though they were 'the invasion' out of the new houses.

Mrs Strong

Windsor Clive School, 1929.

Windsor Clive School, 1932.

5 The Second World War and Austerity

Linda David in her Grand Avenue garden with an Anderson shelter left over from the war.

War and Ely

We were much more parochial then, you didn't know much about what was going on in the world. Your world didn't extend far. You knew of it because they brought some refugees to the Sunday school. I remember the superintendent standing up and saying these little boys were refugees from the war in Spain. In 1938 we all had to go and queue up one Sunday afternoon and get measured for gas masks.

Harry Griffiths

Tony Simmonds in the back garden of the family house in Cowbridge Road. In the distance can be seen Treseders greenhouses and the roof of the Regent cinema.

Anderson shelters

We had the old Anderson shelter out there and we used to pile into that in the night. We lived there during the night and sometime in the day if you heard bombers coming over. Everybody had an Anderson shelter.

Mrs Permintella

Air-raid shelter

We used to have an air raid shelter in the bottom of the garden. My father made a room in there so that everything was down there that we needed. We didn't have to empty the house and run - food, beds and blankets were all there. I was only three then.

Mrs Dollah

Air raids over Ely

In 1938 Red House was to be demolished in order to complete the house building so my family had to move out. We moved to a house in Cowbridge Road which was later to become what is now Ely Conservative Club.

The house became an ARP post and the local members would call in the evening to sign the register. Whenever the air-raid siren sounded myself and my two brothers would be rushed downstairs and put into the Morrison shelter, which was in the centre of the rear living room. Within seconds the air-raid wardens would report for duty. I remember lying in the shelter looking at all these people sitting around waiting for the first bomb to fall. Very soon I would hear the shells going off and bombs exploding, although I didn't realise at the time the danger we were all in.

A battery of guns was stationed on Ely racecourse. With these firing salvos almost continuously the noise was deafening. The following day my brothers would be allowed to go out and pick up shrapnel from the night's raid.

Tony Simmonds

Tony Simmonds with his mother outside their house in Cowbridge Road.

Air-raid precautions

I did a stint at Red House Clinic at the beginning of the war at the first aid post in the Civil Defence. It was voluntary – the Air Raid Precautions wardens, first-aiders and so forth. Boys about fifteen could become voluntary messengers. One or two nights a week you'd sleep up there all night in the bunks. You'd always be being sent on courses; you'd have mock manoeuvres on a Sunday when you'd pretend there had been a major attack and you'd all be running around. We had a little billiard table and darts up there. First I was in the clinic where the first aid and messengers were then to Redhouse Farm where the wardens were based.

Harry Griffiths

Bombs in Ely

One day in the war we went to the Regent and a bomb dropped near The Dusty Forge and apparently absolute mayhem broke out in The Avenue cinema. All the people were trying to get out and everything shook and that. My mother, well they all heard the bomb dropping and my mother was worried sick because she thought we was in The Avenue cinema. The air raid warning had gone off and we had gone down in the shelter and when we came home she was out on the road. She said I heard there was panic and we said, well we didn't go to the Avenue cinema.

Ladies over fifties club, Pethybridge Hall

Moving out of Ely

I was the eldest child and looked after my sister Beryl and brothers Keddie, Dougie and Melvin, the last two being born in Ty Coch Road. Although I did not want to leave them, by the time I was twenty-two I felt I had to get a proper job, even though that meant moving away.

So I left Ely and started work in the Ovaltine factory in King's Langley and was there to see the Battle of Britain being fought out in the skies over London. My connection with fighter planes was to be even closer as I went on to work on the seats and upholstery for Spitfires and Hurricanes in the trim shop of the big upholstery company Cox's. It was there I met my future husband; James Macdonald or Mac as everybody called him, he had come looking for work all the way from Whitley Bay on Tyneside. We settled in Garston, Watford, where we brought up our daughter; Audrey.

Apart from the run in with a car on the Cowbridge Road I had some good memories of Ely, seeing the racehorses on Ely Racecourse and watching them being taken to Llewellyn's stables at the top of the Grand Avenue, at the bottom of which I can remember them building the wooden library. The hardest part was leaving my brothers and sister behind.

Marjorie Elsie Gwendoline Macdonald (née Jones)

Guns and rockets on the racecourse

When the rocket battalions were formed I was one of them. The rocket projectors were managed by the home guard and consisted of seventy-five projectors, which could fire 150 rockets at a time. They were manned by the home guard and we trained at the Penarth Golf Course. Our flash insignia consisted of a black arrow on a red background. At Penarth we would fire out to sea which would make us one of the first rocket sites in the world. There were two men to a projector each one firing two rockets six foot long. The projector consisted of a metal framework with two wheels on it. Two operators were called number one and number two. I was a number one.

I remember the time when MacConeechie, my number two, took off his overcoat to load his rockets. When he looked for it at the end of firing all he could find was a couple of scorched buttons - he must have dropped it where the rocket discharged!

At the entrance to the Racecourse on the right hand side could be found the anti-aircraft battery station, the 3.7 guns with the regular army on the left-hand side. We were allowed to use the NAAFI. In the Nissen huts on the left-hand side, one hut had a trestle table and a barrel of beer – the original Home Guard Club. Before the rocket battalion many of us had joined the local defence volunteers (LDV). Major Evans, the Head of Herbert Thomson, was in charge of us, he had the only revolver, the Sergeant had the only rifle and the rest of us had pickaxe handles.

Mr Williams

The Ely Home Guard

Over the war time period the racecourse was the home of several different Royal Artillery units. Early on, a light field battery was training there. This was followed by a heavy AA unit, which stayed for several years. This was followed by a new introduction the 'Z battery' or 'Rocket Battery'. Rocket Batteries were very heavy on manpower. A Battery consisted of sixty-four twin-barrelled projectors (not guns). These were set out in a formation of eight rows of eight projectors. Each had a crew of four men, a layer, a trainer and two ammunition numbers. This meant that 256 men were required to 'man' the battery before even looking at the various support functions. The Regular army provided the training and fire control functions.

These included an ATS detachment operating the Radar. The Home Guard element was on duty every eighth night.

Volunteer messengers at Red House Clinic during the war.

During the war most civilian-based night duties were done on an eight night basis.

So a fully manned rocket detachment would require well over 2000 men. Whether this was ever fully attained I would not know, but I doubt if Ely Racecourse could manage that number of men.

Jack Julian

Ely Hospital and the War

In the early days of the war the gun crews on Ely racecourse used to come to the hospital for baths and showers. There was nothing over there; they were just in the middle of the racecourse. The windows in the hospital would shake when the guns fired so we had to open every door and window, the noise was so loud. The biggest menace was the fumes.

Later they built concrete shelters (they were built of concrete slabs with steps down underground) but there was still a rule that you had to go, as soon as the warning went, while you were on duty you got a tip off when you heard the alarm bells going on the Ack Ack site before the public warning went. Then we'd get them down the shelters straight away. You might be down there two hours and all the meals would go cold. Then one night a week when you were off duty you had to do fire watching and you got three shillings for that. You slept on the premises and if the warning went you had to go down on the fire escape and watch for incendiary bombs. You know where the Leisure Centre is, there used to be two large hangers there. That was the balloon barrage site – they serviced balloons. The balloons had to be put on cables and sent up to the roof with people alongside to test them.

Mr and Mrs Keays

Guns on Ely racecourse

In my house in those days there was a dresser and on the top shelf was all my best glasses that were only used now and again. The guns were on the racecourse and there was this Scottish company over there. They used to play the bagpipes. It was all dark and still and you could hear this. They used to have these searchlights that used to flash over and then the guns would go off. So the next time I went to wash the top of the dresser all the glasses were cracked.

Ladies over fifties club, Pethybridge Hall

The War and rationing

My first house was in Marcross Road. They dropped a bomb over in the fields not far from where we were.

We did all right on rationing. We'd sell some of our food it'd only go to waste and also some of our clothing coupons. There was an awful lot of it going on. If my mother had no money I used to go over the pawnshop in Canton. We'd take my fathers suit and have three to four shillings. If he had to go anywhere, he had no suit, so I was always the one who had to go down there. He'd have to wait two days. On the shelves were all people's belongings. My mother used to sell his watch as well. I used to hate having to go down there. I used to say mum don't make me go down there.

My mother used to have big cast iron saucepans and made pea soup. She put in lentils, potatoes, bacon bones - allsorts. On Mondays and Fridays we used to go to a house in Archer Crescent for faggots and peas for three pence; Wakeleys it was called. You could buy a jug of gravy. She would cook faggots in one boiler and gravy in the other. Tuppence for a piece of fish and a penny for chips. The first fish shop was Males in Mill Road - they

Lower Grand Avenue at the junction of Phyllis Crescent (later renamed Heol Muston) showing white lines on the lamp-posts, which were to assist in the blackout. The bus shelter and public toilets are on the left.

sold hake. You'd get scraps for nothing (the batter off the fish).

We would have bread and milk before we went to school. There would be a big piece of bread, no slices in those days, in a basin with hot water over it to soften it and some milk and sugar. There used to be a house in Cowbridge Road, nearby the White Lion at the back called the nurses (old mother Cross) where they used to go for dinners. Free meals. The nurse used to look after the kids. If the kid's father wasn't working they used to have dinner tickets.

Mr and Mrs Page

Allotments

I lived at the back of the old library, where the new library is now. They turned it into three allotments; my husband had one, the man next door and a man across The Avenue had the third one. Then our neighbour Mr Slater went out to Burma so my husband did his allotment until he came back.

Ladies over fifties club, Pethybridge Hall

Sailing away – 1942

We lived in Ty Coch Road and one of my earliest memories was of seeing a magic lantern show in the church hall. We also used to go to see the shows at Highmead House, play in Plymouth Woods and watch the horse racing at Ely Racecourse. I went to Herbert Thompson school usually carrying my younger brother Jim home on my back, he was never very well. He was called up as a Royal Marine during the war but the war ended before he saw active service. I went into the Royal Naval Volunteer Reserve, going to Chatham Barracks for training on the Thames. I returned to Cardiff to join my first ship, which I believe was the Hope Crown, and later served a sister ship; the Hope Tarn, and I was to spend two years on the Ocean Pilgrim. Leaving Cardiff we called in at Belfast for repairs before sailing to New York. We had a terrific welcome, America was not yet in the war and crowds were waiting on the dockside in their cars. They wanted to treat us to a good time in Manhattan, even offering to put us up if we wanted to jump ship but everyone went back to the ship. The highlight was visiting Jack Dempsey's gym and watching him train.

Next we went to Hong Kong and crossed over to mainland China, on our return we sailed to India. Round to Malta and on to Port Said, sailing through the Suez Canal and on to Australia. In Freemantle we were given warm clothing for the trip back. We sailed to Cape Town, South Africa, docking in the shadow of the table Top Mountain. Another voyage was to Argentina, which was to remain a neutral country throughout the war. Other countries included Egypt and Burma and then round to Penang. I remember watching the dolphins racing alongside the ship when I was on look out duty at night. Whales could be seen swimming way off in the distance during the day and flying fish would land on the deck. We would pick them up and throw them back over the side if they were still alive. Small birds would rest on the rigging during their long flights over water. At the end of my sailing days we were engaged on coastal work up and down the Thames. I left the RNVR and got a job in the GKN steelworks, where my father worked. He had an accident in the works but continued afterwards, coming into the works on sticks. I worked for GKN until my retirement.

Douglas Jones

The Americans

The Americans were everywhere. There was a lot of feelings you know, because a lot of girls were left on their own and it was a great temptation. Fortunately I had a young fella. You must get very lonely when there is nothing to do. Once they left the country they didn't know when, or if, they were coming back. When you think how many men were killed in that war needlessly… dreadful.

Ladies over fifties club, Pethybridge Hall

The Communists

At that time there were a few famous Russian generals, one was called Timoshenko and the yarn going round, and we believed this, was that he was descended from a Welshman called Timothy Jenkins. All the propaganda was pro-Russian in the news. Communists were still regarded with great suspicion. A chap I knew joined the Young Communist League and not long after the police came to his house and asked to see his father and asked him did you know that your son is in the Young Communists and works in the post office for the government.

Harry Griffiths

Clearing snow the American way

The Americans were over in the quarry at the bottom of Plymouthwood Road. There were a couple of hundred of them. They used to give us sweets and clear all the snow up here. We would laugh at them. Once we were snowed in, we couldn't get out, it was terrible. Then one night we heard a terrible noise. We said, 'Oh! the Americans are here.' They had their bulldozers to clear it. Where the Herbert Thomson school is now that's where the Americans were; they even had showers.

Mr and Mrs Page

Catherine Steadman outside her house in Marcross Road. The windows are taped to provide protection from bomb blasts.

WHERE DO **YOU** BUY YOUR

BUTTER BACON CHEESE SUNDRIES?

IF YOU DO NOT BUY THESE AT THE WEST END STORES

YOU MISS THE JOY OF LIVING!

We do not sell everything, but what we do sell carries with it our personal Guarantee of CLEANLINESS, QUALITY, and ABSOLUTE SATISFACTION.

ALWAYS AT YOUR SERVICE.

THE WEST END STORES

The Store which gives you personal attention. (CARDIFF) LTD

65 THE GRAND AVENUE,
58 PETHYBRIDGE ROAD,
ELY.

39 ST. FAGANS ROAD,
2 FAIRWATER GREEN,
FAIRWATER.

West End Stores advert August 1940.

Wartime dances

I can remember the American soldiers marching up the street here. Most of them were black. Up in Llandaff the American Military Police were stationed and they used to send out invitations to all the local hospitals to any of their dances. So many nurses could go and they always sent transport for them. The nurses were very popular but they had to be in by eleven o'clock. There would be jeeps, three-tonners and armoured cars bringing them back at night to Ely Hospital. No yellow lines in those days!!

I remember the machine-gunning of a train passing by the Paper Mill. I was on the ward alone with about sixty patients. That was 1944.

Mr and Mrs Keays

Prisoners of War

I remember the Polish guards down the bottom of the Avenue, very stern looking men, and the German soldiers sweeping the snow. The Italians were up the Drope in the summer. They were gorgeous looking fellas!

Ladies over fifties club, Pethybridge Hall

Escaped POWS

I first came across the Italian POW's in about 1945 when I was working for the Executive at Culverhouse Cross and they used to work alongside us then. They all had big circles for some reason stuck on the back of their jackets. They were 'co operators' as they were called. They lived in a big camp the other side of Wenvoe - a big Italian camp. They used to ride round Ely on bikes when they weren't working - chasing the girls and all sorts. They were absolutely free really.

The Germans were down in Island Farm in Bridgend. They broke out, I remember that really well, I was going to work. I was working down the mines by this time. I was catching a bus to the station from Grand Avenue and the army stopped the bus just the other side of Ely roundabout. They made us all get off and had a good look at us all. That was what it was all about. Two hundred Germans had escaped. There was a few Germans working up on the agricultural project on the land; one guard used to come with them.

Harry Griffiths

Working during the War

My first job in Ely was at the Paper Mills where most of Ely seemed to work! Most of the women working there had long hair and had to wear a kind of hairnet called a snood – I remember my mother telling us that she was one of the first in Cardiff to have a bob cut. With the outbreak of war a lot of the men were being called up and they relied on women to make up the workforce. I wanted to join up myself and join the WRENS. My boss said I could not go but I was determined to and signed up for two years, which upset my boss who told me not to come back here looking for a job. My father was also against me joining up, threatening that I would not have a home to come back to if I did. But I went, being stationed in Mill Hill in London, and despite being my first time away from Cardiff, enjoyed it – except for being shook up by all the doodle bombs.

I left the WRENS with some great memories and a medal and came back to Cardiff where I went to work in Littlewoods Pools in St Mary Street. This was not for me and I decided that I would get my old job back in the Paper Mill and went to see my old boss; Mr Snook, he asked me what did I want and I said my old job please. He smiled and said start tomorrow! Jobs were so easy to get then. I met Ken Jones, whose real name was Kedwyn but everyone called him Ken or Keddie, just after he got demobbed from the Army. He lived in Ely before the war and started working as a driver for Ross Transport in Bute Road, and we courted and got engaged on my twenty-first birthday. We were married when I was twenty-two and went to Eastbourne for our honeymoon. There I visited my former CO; Lt Commander Cann, who had lost a hand in the war and one of my first jobs in the WRENS was to help him with his false hand. When he heard I had married an Army man he was disgusted saying that there was plenty of sailors to choose from! We came back to Cardiff and lived in Cathays and Llanishen, having two children there; Maria and Stephen, before coming back to Ely and bringing them and two more children; Stuart and Vincent up in Heol Carnau.

Doreen Jones (née Steadman)

Celebrations and the War

Remember the outings in the street? We used to celebrate anything. We didn't have royal weddings then. We had the Silver Jubilee of King George V and we had a bar of chocolate in school. Then we had the coronation when the old fella died. Then on top of that we had the war and when anyone came home we had a big party. People were coming home all the time especially when the war ended. We had bonfires up and down the streets for weeks; we had all the streets decorated up. For a month it went on.

My brother came home – he'd been away six years. When he went away I was twelve and eighteen when he came home. I always remember going to the station to meet him and he walked past me. He didn't know me. He had an Australian hat on, it was wonderful. I used to ask him to take me to town just so I could walk with him wearing that hat.

Ladies over fifties club, Pethybridge Hall

Ely Paper Mill workers during the war. Doreen Jones is peering over heads, back middle.

VE day party

When we had the party on VE day that was the first one, about six of us made a little committee up and we went round and collected one teaspoon for the tea and one teaspoon for the sugar.

I went out to Albany Road to get some gelatine and that was a long way then on the buses. We had a couple of bottles of pop. We made the jelly in those big brown bowls. That night, well it was about two in the morning and people had gone to bed, they were running down the street shouting, 'the war is over, the war is over'.

We listened on the radio. It said Germany had surrendered and all of a sudden all over the lights started going on and people started bringing out kitchen chairs in the middle of the road. It was absolutely marvellous. Everywhere you walked around people were dancing about. The next party quite a lot of woman put their wedding dresses on, we were all so slim after all the rationing that they could all get in to their dresses.

Ladies over fifties club, Pethybridge Hall

After the War

We went to Windsor Clive school, Bobby Tobin got beri beri as a Japanese Prisoner of War. Before the war he played for Cardiff City but he couldn't play after the war because he couldn't see the ball above his head. I worked as a butcher boy for seven shillings and sixpence per week in Pooles, now Dewhurst, on Wilson Road. I then went to work at

Chivers but once I reached sixteen they let me go because they wouldn't pay adult wages. Then after nine months off I worked in the quarry (the Alps) – it was slave labour!

Eventually I got a job in Brains earning 25s a week driving lorries.

There were stables where there are flats now in Green Farm Road, the stables were burnt down during the war when they used to store films, the fire burnt for two days, the old wall is still there. Squatters took over the old Nissen huts on Ely Racecourse - some soldiers made it their home.

Mr H. Watkins

Building houses in south Ely

At the end of the war I married Tom Cumner, who I had met during my nursing training in Dartford, Kent. Owing to the housing shortage we lived with my mother in rooms in Newport Road. Our son Paul was born there and with the birth of my daughter Christine in 1949 we were given a house in Stanway Road, Ely, we couldn't believe our luck.

We spent nearly two years there amongst friendly neighbours and were very happy. At that time they were building houses in other parts of Ely, on the racecourse and around Cwrt yr Ala Road. We applied for and got a house in Heol Yr Odyn where I still live today. I brought up my family in this house, as the saying goes 'New house, new baby', as in 1952 my daughter Siân was born. All the neighbours moved in together around the same time, and all had young children, it was very hard for many years, the houses were cold. We moved into the house in December 1950, it snowed heavy that winter, we had no street lighting, pavements or roads so when it rained or snowed we were up to our ankles in mud.

Muriel Cumner

Childrens Street Party, Parker Place, 1945.

Celebrating the end of the war in Europe at a VE Party in Haig Place (Cowbridge Road West is behind the hedge, with Sweldon Hill beyond).

Working on the land

The quarry was at Plymouthwood Road and was partially filled in as I remember. At the end of the war I worked for what they called the Glamorgan War Agricultural Executive, every county had one; they ploughed up as much land as they could. All the land where Tesco is now at Culverhouse. It was originally Culverhouse Farm but they took it over.

Harry Griffiths

Ely Brewery

At the start of the Second World War I bought a house and went over to shift work because the pay was better. The night shifts were from five in the morning until one in the afternoon and from midnight to seven in the morning. On Saturdays they went from noon to nine and nine to the following morning. One man was on at the time and you had to keep the pressure up in the two boilers which involved going up five flights of stairs each time.

The first shift meant cleaning out loads of copper vessels that the beer had been in using a brush and silver sand. Apart from seeing to the boilers five massive tanks of water had to be brought to the boil ready for brewing in the morning. Beer that had been boiled in the morning was turned out into cast iron vessels and pumped upwards to cool it. It was then refrigerated. In the tun room it would be seventy degrees Fahrenheit. Yeast would be mixed with the beer and on the third morning after it had finished fermenting it would be pumped from there but kept at sixty-nine degrees until it was needed for the barrels.

On the midnight shift the first job was to clean the copper fire out and wheel up half a dozen barrows of coal ready for the men to start in the morning. Then the cast iron vessels had to be emptied of the hops that were left after the beer had been drained away. After these jobs were finished we would go to the tun room where the beer was in wooden vats, mixed with yeast, and rouse it up. There were four vats, which had to be done at different times. By about four in the morning the vats would have a big head of scum, which had to be skimmed off with an aluminium skimmer.

Beer from the fermenting room was pumped to the settling back room. Here there were pipes, called temperators, which circulated the big containers of beer and kept it to a certain heat. The ten to twelve containers had to be checked every hour. Often I would be running with sweat. My friends who didn't work in the brewery often

Ely Brewery workers in the early 1950s.

VE Party, Caerau Lane, 1945. Nissen huts of RAF Llandaff can be seen in the background.

said they envied me my job because at least I was able to drink on the job but I never drank at night. I preferred tea.

Ernest Strong

The Regent

No memories of lower Ely would be complete without mentioning the Regent cinema. This provided the main form of entertainment in Ely during and after the war. In spite of the many power cuts the audience would be kept entertained by the manager conducting community singing. It was sad when it was converted to a bingo hall and even sadder when it was pulled down.

Tony Simmonds

Squatting in the Ely race-course

When I first got married we lived in rooms in Canton but we were not happy with them and were looking for other accommodation. About two years after getting married we moved in with my mother in Ely. It was at this time that I heard that there was some empty Nissen huts on the old racecourse and that people were squatting there.

With my brother I rushed down to the racecourse and put my name on one of the huts. I was one of the first so I was able to choose a hut with a toilet attached. Housing was scarce at the time so the couples who squatted were very glad to have their own places.

The huts were pretty basic when people first moved in. Oil lamps were used although there was electricity in the form of overhead cables. There was a central hut referred to as 'ablutions', which initially had showers and basins. Water was fetched from there although some of the cleverer men arranged for pipes to run to their huts. The basins were taken out and put in people's huts.

After about six months Cardiff Corporation recognised the squatters and became their landlord. Proper sinks and water were installed and the electricity supply improved but it was insufficient for cookers so the Corporation supplied coal-fired stoves. I used a primus stove as well mainly for the kettle. The rent as far as I can remember was seven shillings and six pence. On one occasion a military gentleman, possibly an officer, came over from another camp that was also on the racecourse. He was very encouraging and said he hoped we would all be happy there. He noticed some people had discarded the cork lino and fitted ordinary lino. He advised me against doing that as he said the concrete floor sweated and would ruin ordinary lino.

Because the hut was one big room my uncle who was a joiner built low partitions to divide it up into a kitchen, best room and bedroom. These partitions were later replaced by corporation workmen who also cut a window in the middle of the hut, for the central room, which because of the new partitions went up to the roof had no source of light. There was an old fashioned round stove left by the previous occupants. I was really proud of my garden. I grew vegetables and kept ducks and chickens. An old shower base taken from the 'ablutions' formed a duck pond. Everyone put in a great effort both inside and outside their huts. It was marvellous. We worked very hard on them and people used to come and were amazed. For my washing I used to heat water, both on the stove and the primus, and fill an old boiler, then scrub the clothes with a rubbing board. On bath night we used a zinc bath.

By the end of the forties the council were housing the families and as people moved out workman moved in to demolish the huts and tear up the concrete bases. They built Trelai school on the site. Eventually in the summer of 1950 only two couples without children were left although I was pregnant by then. There was a question mark over whether we were going to get a house until it was pointed out at a council meeting that an undertaking had been given to re-house all the squatters. So we moved to a council house in Ely. I cried for a month after I moved. I felt so penned in. The house seemed so small and I missed the freedom of the fields. It was really wonderful living there.

Mrs Dodd

Prefab in Heol-yr-Odyn, late 1940s.

Snow

In 1947 we had heavy snow. Everybody dug down the road to the corner shop, there were mazes of walkways.

Mrs Permintella

Trelai hall

Mr Llewellyn used to go round the doors selling these little football tickets to get funds, to get enough money, to start the place off and build a hall. This was about 1948/49.

Mr Rolands

Above and below: Squatting on Ely racecourse after the Second World War.

Children of families squatting on Ely racecourse after the Second World War.

Trelai Hall, 10 February 2002.

6 Towards the Millennium!

Model of the new bottlery, with the model maker Mr Lark, front right, 4 June 1958.

Foundation Stone Laying of New Ely Brewery Bottling Store

The sun made a welcome return to Cardiff to shine auspiciously on the scene as Mr Lazarus Nidditch, chairman and managing director, laid the foundation stone of the Ely Brewery Companys new bottling store on Monday 9 June 1958.

Dr J. Saper the vice-chairman said, 'The increasing demand for our bottled beers which made the greater output provided by this new store essential is directly due to the personal efforts of the Chairman'.

Underneath the stone Mr Nidditch had previously placed a set of coins and some Coronation medallions distributed by the company at the time to staff and shareholders. He went on to say that, 'I am confident that

The foundation stone being laid by Mr L Nidditch, 4 June 1958 .

this bottlery will not only be a great asset to Ely Brewery but also a valuable addition to the future industry of Cardiff'.

'Mild and Bitter' the Ely Brewery house magazine, Summer 1958

Ely Brewery

When Ely Brewery was taken over books and furniture was brought to Ely to be destroyed. It was a pitiful sight.

I was one of the last to leave the old brewery because I saw to the boiler and by the time I moved to the new site Whitbreads were negotiating to take over. I worked in the boiler house until I retired in 1968 but the work had changed completely by then; coal had been replaced by oil and it was completely automated.

Ernest Strong

Caerau Square

War broke out; our sons were called to war and some never returned. D Day arrived and neighbours got together for our street tea. One prisoner of war returned. Vicar Evans

Ely brewery workers, late 1950s to early 1960s.

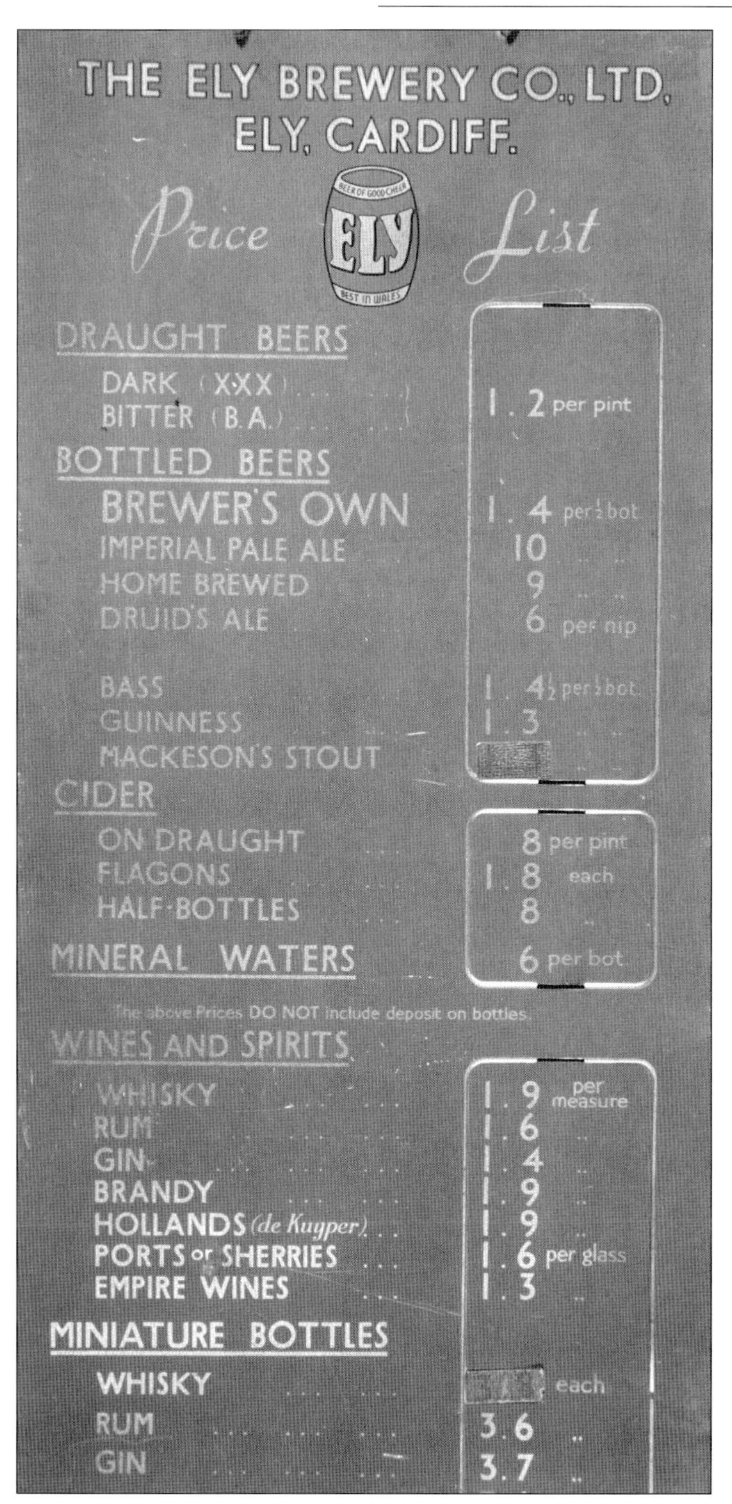

Ely Brewery price list 1950s.

Caerau Square, 1938.

was the guest of honour.

Then new houses were being built all over Cardiff and one by one the people left the square. Our rent in those days was ten shillings and three pence. The bulldozers came and knocked the houses down. New ones were built and in came the new neighbours. Caerau Square was renamed St David's Crescent.

Mrs Tompkins

Plymouth woods

The youths of even twenty years ago will remember Plymouth woods and the river in all its glory. Bathing in the river was a delightful pastime; a fire was essential to dry off by, as most participants did not have parental approval. Some did not possess bathing trunks - underpants were the normal wear and it was not unknown for even those to be discarded. An efficient alternative was a tea towel tied nappy fashion. Girls were banned from the bathing area except those with their mothers. Places round the fire were

Caerau Square in the process of being demolished, 1962.

acquired strictly in precedence of age. Sometimes a girl would manage to get in for a swim but they were never really welcomed only tolerated.

The woods was a very special adventure playground – monkey trees to climb on, logs to swing on and hills to scramble on, bracken and bramble for den making and a real swamp to loose ones shoes in. Trains passing by - to wave and make rude faces to. It's easy to poke your tongue out when there is no chance of getting caught. Patients at the nearby but inaccessible TB hospital were wheeled out to the veranda every day except when it rained. They enjoyed our waves, which was their only social contact.

Money was scarce so mums would pack food and drink for the day and congregate at their favourite place – second or third bridge, St Fagans crossing or even the Drope if the mum felt energetic. The day was crowned with a game of rounders with all the mums joining in. To call in the farm for a glass of goat's milk on the way home was an experience never really appreciated until you look back.

Another great adventure was the day when mum decided it was the right time for 'blue-belling'. Then apprehensively awaiting the yell of 'parkee' and running non stop with the blue trophies, armfuls of blue bells to be distributed among the elderly neighbours. Although this was an event enacted by many people year after year the blue bell dell was never abused and retained its glory year after year.

Alma Cridland

Keeping children amused!

There were quite a number of children around then when we moved in, they had quite a good childhood, used to play altogether in the street (that was when the roads were built) and very little traffic. They spent a lot of their time up the woods, on Cwrt-yr-Ala park, and walk to 'Blue Water' and 'Jackdaw Island' and would go off for most of the day. Then in blackberry season, they used to pick them and sell them to Chivers, near Ely Bridge, with the money they earned they'd go to Cold Knap and swim in the open-air swimming baths. When it snowed they all used to take a lid of a tin, walk to Spillers Hill and slide down. They'd have fun up there for hours and come back soaking wet and cold.

Muriel Cumner

Supply teaching

I retired in July 1967 but for twenty years before that I was head of a nursery school in Vachell Road. I had taught girls and boys but

Bluebell collecting in Plymouth woods.

never nursery. I was working somewhere in Grangetown on supply. I went back in the wartime and was put all over the place on supply. A note came round one day asking if anybody was interested in nursery teaching. I forgot all about it. I was in another school by then and children would go to Porthcawl for a fortnight with a teacher. I would go and take the remainder of the class. On supply you got paid eight shillings for a morning and the same for an afternoon. You were paid for the actual time you were in school. It was dreadful really. If you worked hard in those days you used to get half a day a month good attendance. If you worked like a slave all the month to get good attendance you would get paid a little extra.

Mrs Strong

Teaching in Ely

My father Fred Croster (Crosta) organised many sporting activities for the youth of Ely. Around 1939 he ran a Boxing and Boys Club in Archer Road. When he returned from Germany after the war he became a teacher of physical education at Cyntwell Secondary school. Also, at this time he became very involved with Welsh Rugby and for many years was on the Cardiff Committee. He later became an International Rugby Referee. He was well known for measuring the distance covered by a referee in a rugby match using a pedometer.

Sue Blain (née Croster)

Shopping in Ely

Around 1946 my grandparents Alfred and Winnifred Crosta lived in Phyllis Crescent, now known as Heol Muston. My grandmother ran a very small shop from the hall in the house, selling anything from sweets to household items, much like a general store. She was well known for making Dandelion and Burdock, Nettle Cordial and other herbal drinks, which she may have sold. My grandfather used the garden shed to store newspapers, which he delivered to customers. He also bought and delivered fish. When the new shops were built in Bishopston Road to serve the South Ely estate around 1951/52, they moved and opened Crosta's Newsagents. Many of the older residents of Ely will remember my grandfather as a very serious looking man who always smoked a pipe. They stayed there until they retired.

Sue Blain (née Croster)

Trolleybuses

My last main recollection of Ely was when the trolleybuses came in May 1955. Being a trolleybus enthusiast I watched with great interest the construction of the overhead throughout the winter of 1954/55. Sadly the system was only to last fifteen years.

Tony Simmonds

A trick on the trolleybus

I used to work on the trolley buses. We used to have tricks. If you wanted a couple of hours off, on the wires there was junction boxes and if you hit the wire hard enough with the pole it used to knock the head off. That was it. Terrible I know!!

Mrs Dollah

Ely Hospital

Ely enquiry: Headline on three o'clock news. We couldn't believe it was the place we'd worked in. We drove straight to the hospital and found about twelve people had done the same. The day after the report came out they

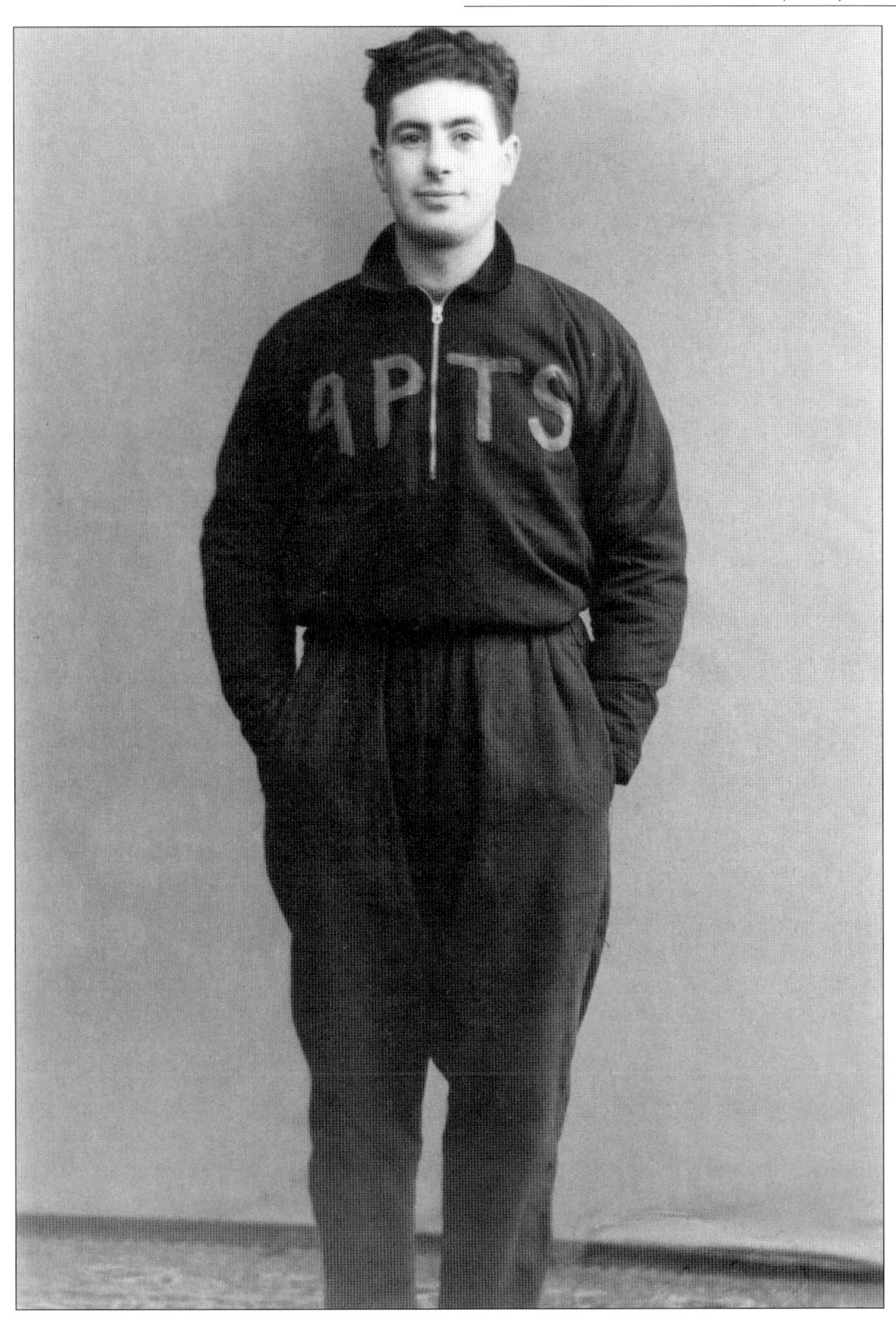

Fred Croster, Army Physical Training Instructor and later Physical Education teacher at Cyntwell High School.

The Crosta family. Back row: Fred, Terence and Ken. Front row: Pop and Mam Crosta, Gloria and Phillip. In the background can be seen the flats on Heol Trelai.

Pop Crosta in his Bishopston Road shop.

Double and single deck trolleybuses, Macdonald Road.

Trolleybus at the bottom of Grand Avenue (note two-way traffic on one lane).

Ely Hospital, early 1980s, showing the original Ely Industrial school frontage which was built in 1862 and opened in 1863.

137 years of Ely Hospital; an existing reminder in Summer 2000. The gateway now provides access to retail units including another German connection on the site; Aldi's! *(See 'The Hess legend' on p.25).*

laid carpets in every ward. They gave me £1000 to go into town and buy toys for my ward. The day after they came the carpet was taken up, believe it or not. The toys stayed.

They were self-sufficient. All the patients who were capable of work used to work on the garden and I must say they loved it. They would sell a lot of green vegetables and other produce to the Infirmary and Whitchurch. I remember a couple of women in there who were simply put in there because they were single girls who had babies

There was barbed wire on the wall that runs up by Arles Road to stop people getting in but of course they filmed it from a low angle and said it was a concentration camp. It was to stop the local teenagers getting on the wall because they used to tease the patients so the barbed wire was to stop them.

They had an Occupational Therapy department that was closed down after the NHS took over. It was really productive; they used to make chain link fencing, mats, scrubbing brushes, carpets and all done by hand by the patients. They would last a lifetime.

You'd take twelve patients to Ninian Park on a Saturday to see the City; you'd walk there and back no matter what the weather. You try and watch twelve. I lost quite a few. It was in the days when City were in their prime. The average gate was 30-40,000. We went into the player's entrance and not through the turnstiles.

Mr and Mrs Keays

Headlines

The day the news came about the allegations at the Hospital, the British army invaded Anguilla. It was a cover up - everyone said that. It was headlines on the three o'clock news.

Mr and Mrs Keays

Johnny Blain and the youth club

The Youth Club on Ely racecourse was run by my father, Johnny Blain, in the 1950s. He had moved to Cardiff after the Second World War, being born in Toxteth, Liverpool in 1915. Known to everyone as 'Johnny' he ran the club at Trelai School especially for youngsters aged thirteen to nineteen years. The teenagers would take part in activities such as sport, music and dance, and rock and roll nights were held regularly. At first there was a skiffle group and then later on a rhythm group called the 'Alley Cats'. The youth club had a big following and there was great disappointment when it closed down in 1957 and moved to the 'Vic' Ballroom in Canton. My father died in 1994 aged seventy-nine years.

Phil Blain

Highfields

Where the Highfields pub is it used to be an old farmhouse where Mr Crowley lived. He opened it up as a store for groceries for people living in the prefabs. Further down from him was two old gents in a farm; they used to sell groceries and potatoes, swede and other vegetables.

Mr Rolands

Johnny Blain as Al Jolson 1958.

The Millward brothers; Gomer, Jeff and Eric.

Millwards piggery

At the back of our house in Heol yr Odyn we had Millwards the pig farm. There were three brothers, Gomer, Eric and Jeff. They kept around 450 pigs, which were kept spotless. The brothers were all friendly and helpful and were a part of the community.

My children used to wake up to the sound of the pigs squealing or geese screeching and the guard dog was named Teddy whom everyone loved. It was like living right in the heart of the countryside and we loved it. We were sorry when Millwards left. Now it is the site of Lauriston Park.

Muriel Cumner

Shopping in Caerau

We had no facilities, only a small shop in Caerau called Abletts where we could get our rations. Then sometime later we had a Co-op travelling shop for our groceries, a butcher, and a green grocer from Grangetown named George Stenner. The highlight of the week was when they arrived and we got to know our neighbours and have a chat and a laugh.

Muriel Cumner

Wheatsheaf club

There used to be the Wheatsheaf Recreation

Ground behind us in Amroth Road. It was very pleasant in summer time: they used to play cricket and football on the ground. The pavilion got set on fire and they decided to sell the ground to the Corporation.

Mr Rolands

Shops in Old Ely

After the war when things got more or less back to normal I was at the age of eight allowed my first taste of freedom. I could now move around the local area and get to know the places and its people.

Next door to the Conservative Club was Knights Transport Café. There was always a long line of lorries parked outside while the drivers took their break; something that would be impossible now.

A little further down the road just past the British Legion Club was a small shop, run by a very old deaf lady named Miss Willis. Her shop was always empty including the shelves. However she did sell very nice ice lollies which she would remove from an otherwise empty old fashioned fridge in the rear room. They were just one penny in price.

On the corner of Mill Road stood the White Lion pub, which was run my Mr and Mrs Mahoney. Although the smell emitting from there was very attractive it was a place my parents strongly advised me to keep clear of.

Next along Mill Road was a haberdashery shop run by Miss James, then a small fish and chip shop run by Mrs Male. Across the road was Davies's snack bar that also sold delicious ice lollies while opposite was Shaplands clothes store followed by a sweet shop and an ironmongers.

Next to the ironmongers was the gents barbers run by Mr Hitchins. I was always sent to him for a hair-cut but I didn't like this because the shop was filthy and stank of cigarettes. All around were old tins and saucers full to overflowing with cigarette butts. As soon as he finished one he'd light another. As

Cooperative sports day on Wheatsheaf Recreation Ground, 1957.

Miss Wilson's shop.

he cut hair the ash would fall everywhere with the result that customers came away needing a wash and brush up!

The post office was run by Mrs Danks; a large lady with an enormous crop of red hair. Opposite was Miss Peach's newsagent where we got all our papers and on the other side of the lane was Wilson's sweet shop.

A few doors up from there was England's shoe shop which I remember was very dark and had a large bell that rang loudly when the front door opened. Fifty yards up was Palmers the florist on the corner of Colin Way, then Dr O'Shea's and D. Thomas's. Back across the road was Worrels garage and petrol station then Flynn's grocery stores. Moving back down the main road came Treseder's greengrocery shop. All the produce sold there came from the large market garden behind the shop.

Tony Simmonds

Going to the pictures

My memories of the pictures are going to the Avenue Cinema in the mid-fifties and joining the Saturday morning rush - known as the tanner rush. On arrival, the De Bono brothers and I would join the queue, which was the whole length of the cinema and some three or four deep. After paying your tanner (2 1/2p) and buying some pop and sweets you entered the mad house of excited youngsters, where you had about a two hour programme of films. This usually included cartoons, the Three Stooges (my favourite) and a cowboy. The cowboy was always met with cheers for the goodies and boos for the baddies, so there were many boos throughout the film. If the film broke down (which it often did) everybody would stamp their feet until the film was repaired.

The last film was always *Batman & Robin* or

AVENUE, ELY		AVENUE, ELY	
Open 3.45	Wed. 2.0	Open 4.35	Sat. 2.0
KENNETH MORE	KAY KENDALL	CINEMASCOPE	COLOUR
"GENEVIEVE"		ROSSANNA PODESTA	JACK SERNAS
(Wed. 2.20) 5.35 8.50 Tech.	U	HELEN OF TROY	
DIRK BOGARDE	MURIEL PAVLOW	(Sat. 2.55) 5.40 8.25	U
DOCTOR IN THE HOUSE		The Case of the Bogus Count	
3.55 7.10 Tech.	U	(Sat. 2.10) 4.55 7.35	U

Two advertisements for The Avenue, Ely, 29 September 1956.

Flash Gordon and the end of the episode was always a cliff hanger, where the hero would be left in a no win situation, but when you returned the following Saturday for the next part they would always get out of the life threatening problem much to our amazement, it was years later that I realised they changed the ending of the film from the previous week. When the show was over the doors would open and we would rush out blinded by the daylight, with our macs tied around our necks like Batman's cape. We would dive into the hedges of the Western Welsh Bus Depot opposite the cinema, becoming the heroes we had just watched.

Paul Cumner

Caerau (Ely) AFC

Caerau (Ely) was formed in 1955 when it joined the Junior Division of the Cardiff Combination League. A set of red jerseys were given to the club by Mr Ron Miller of Cross Bros AFC and this gift was to determine the colours of the club forever.

In the early years of the club games were played at Ely Racecourse, moving on to Glyn Derw School during the 1980s. In the formative years the secretary Algy David helped steer the club up through the divisions of the Combination League. During the period 1955-1998 the club won almost eighty League and Cup Trophies.

David Guy

Flying away – 1966

When my daughter; Muriel, moved into her first house in Stanway Road, Ely, with her husband Tom and son Paul, I moved in with them. In 1950 we moved to a new house in Heol yr Odyn and I became very involved with Saintwell chapel, then on Cowbridge Road, but which was to move to the new church on Heol Trelai. My son, Cyril or Bob as he preferred to be called, had emigrated from Britain, at first to Canada and then to the United States. In 1966 he arranged for me to fly out and see him. So on the 5 July 1966 my son in law, along with my daughter and granddaughter Siân, took me in his car to London Airport. We set out at three thirty in the morning and got to the airport at eight o' clock.. It was the first time I had flown and I was very nervous. We started off at eleven fifty-five on a flight to Toronto where I was met by my son, we stayed the night with friends and started for Ohio at nine thirty n the morning and reached there at seven o'clock, it took us as much time to go from Toronto to Ohio as it

Caerau (Ely) AFC in 1955.

did from London Airport to America. We went through Ontario where we got out and saw the Niagara Falls, it was beautiful and worth seeing.

We went through Pennsylvania, then to New York States, and there I had to show my passport and Visa to enter America. Eventually we reached my son's house. There is plenty of everything here, they eat what they like, have it when you like and you can do as you like, that's how they live and everyone is so friendly. On Wednesday evening we went to an American ladies birthday party, it was great. I don't like all the sort of food as we are not used to it, but it is very tasty. They also live well out here; we have television from 7 p.m. until three o'clock next morning. If you want your neighbour across the road for anything, perhaps to do your hair, you never go over and ask her, you just phone and she does the same, the phone is ringing nearly all the day.

There are ninety million cars in the States and it is compulsory to have a safety belt. The cars are massive, my son's car holds three in front and four behind and enough room for six children at the back. When you go to the bank to change a cheque you don't get out of the car, outside the bank there is a window with a lady there, you just put your cheque in a drawer and she takes it, and out comes your money. This is the only country that you go in your car to get your employment pay. There is also a drive-in movie, the film starts at ten o'clock when it's dark, and it goes on until three in the morning, you take all your drinks in a cooler and all you want to eat, you pay for each car. When you have visitors we never take them into the house we take them on to the lawn, then we have food and stay out there until about eleven o'clock. The children here don't get so much freedom as our children, they don't pop on a bus for the pictures or a dance, everything is so far away and when they are seventeen they have a car.

Elizabeth (Danny) Daniel

Closure of Chivers

I don't know what I am going to do now the factory is closing. I am only a pickle girl.

The last pickle factory worker

Working in Ely

When my three children got older I went back to work and became a member of the nursing staff in Caerau Hospital, which was five minutes walk up the lane from our house.

I worked there for seventeen years and the majority of the staff were friends and neighbours. We all worked together well, some in the hospital and some in nearby Caerau House, where Sister Duffy was in charge of us. She was very strict and a disciplinarian, the standard of nursing care and cleanliness of the hospital was above reproach. We were all very sad when it closed in 1972 and we were transferred to Ely Hospital and Lansdowne. I stayed in Lansdowne for two years then went to work at the Trelai Adult Day Centre, where I stayed until retirement to look after my husband Tom, in 1979. My husband Tom Cumner was an insurance man for the Royal London and his biggest round was in Ely. Sadly he died in 1980, but many people still remember him wearing his cap and riding his bike or driving his car around the area. We were also well known in the RAFA Club by Ely River, where I'm still a member today.

Muriel Cumner

Sweldon Farm

There was always mixed farming at Sweldon and many cups were won for prize bulls and

Chivers label.

Aerial view showing the former site of Sweldon Farm, mid 1980s. In the centre is Cyntwell High School which later became part of Mostyn Roman Catholic High School and more recently Mary Immaculate. The site of the farm was immediately behind the school (the school itself was demolished at the end of 2001 for housing development).

shire horses at local shows. The lands belonging to the farm took in what later became Ely racecourse and Mostyn Roman Catholic schools playing fields used to be the market garden. I left the farm in 1979; the new link road was the final straw and I decided to give up. The farm buildings were then demolished.

Mrs E.M. Emerson

Community work

I started working in Ely in 1975 as a social worker attached to the Barnardos Family Centre in Ely. The Centre manager was Phyllis Watters who retired on 24 May 2002 after working for over thirty years in Ely. In December 1976 my work changed as I became more involved within community projects.

The Ely Community Shop staff on the tenth anniversary, with Shirley Collins from Ely Citizens Advice Bureau far left, summer 1988.

Overleaf: Caerau playscheme, summer 1978, with Gaynor Lougher and Nigel Billingham on pirate day. Photographed from the field adjacent to the Caerau Infants School.

I had organised my first children's 'playscheme' in Caerau Infants school in 1975, when we coped with 300 children in the hall! The Ely Community Shop opened in Jacrow Square in June 1978, sharing the premises with the Citizens Advice Bureau managed by Shirley Collins. By 1984 the two organisations had moved to 36 Caerau Lane. The 'Shop' was the base for a whole range of different initiatives including a photographer in residence. Martin Roberts held this post for over ten years and many local people had the opportunity to learn photography.

One part of the community work was the Ely Old and New Photographic Exhibition. Five years were spent collecting and copying photographs and listening to peoples' reminiscences. The first exhibition took place in 1984 in Trelai Youth Club, where hundreds of people came to view the exhibition, reminisce and share memories. This exciting project was the starting point for this book and our two previous books on the Ely area.

Nigel Billingham